TO HAVE AND TO HOLD

Keeping Our Marriage Vows

Ngozi Martin-Oguike

ISBN: 9798597458397

* *Dortin Family Series* *

7 Woodbridge Ave,
Sewaren, New Jersey, 07077

Formatted by
BookMarkers
onagwa@gmail.com, 234-805-513-9010

Citations from KJV, NKJV and
The Book of Common Prayer, 1662 and 1928.

I

Table of Contents

To Martin,

For 30 years of fondness,

For trusting God along with me,

For many more years of God's love.

Disclaimer

The scenarios and examples used in this book came from real life events. However, all identifying traits have been hidden; therefore, the names and descriptions of the real characters have been changed to protect the privacy of those involved. As such, any coincidence of name or event within and between the stories and any known person or family are strictly unintentional.

Acknowledgements

When I started studying the efficacy of our marriage vows, it was meant for personal growth; to enrich my marriage experience. However, after some invitations to speak on the subject, I felt the urge to study more. That led to studying other marriages. This study has grown into a book that could be shared with the world around us.

I have learned quite a lot from interactions with different families. Therefore, I appreciate all of you who have in one way or the other enriched my Christian walk. I am grateful to the pastors and churches, among whom we have ministered and still minister.

I want to particularly acknowledge Rev. Samuel Abegunde (of blessed memory) and Pastor Mrs. Bernice Abegunde of the Liberty Evangelical Church, Philadelphia, Pennsylvania; Rev. and Mrs. John Adegoke of Word House Christian Center, Bellmawr, New Jersey; as well as Rev. Canon and Mrs. Linus Amonu of St. Peter's Igbo Church, Trenton, New Jersey, who all provided us opportunities to hold seminars with their congregations on related topics, thus helping us to study and learn along with them. I also thank Dr. Mrs. Florence Eghosa Unuigbe for reading my early manuscript and asking relevant questions.

My sister and friend, Mrs. Lorna Akabogu is very highly appreciated for proofreading and discussing salient points from her own perspective. She helps to bring balance in my renditions. I am grateful to her and her husband, Pastor Christian Akobogu, for their work and ministry among us.

Dr. Godfrey Onagwa of the BookMarkers Publishing Company, Ibadan, Nigeria took time to edit and format the final manuscript in readiness for publishing. Thank you for your diligence.

I couldn't do this without my family crew of multiple-talented men and women. I want to acknowledge my son, Mr. Praise Martin-Oguike, my book cover designer and publishing assistant. I am also grateful to my beloved daughter in-law, Eva-Astoria for diligently proofreading the initial writing with her eagle's eyes. Thanks also for your excitement about the content of the book and desire to have it read by other young couples. Thanks to my daughter, Precious and her husband, Chinwendu, my ferocious readers, whose conversations on this subject greatly impacted this study. Thanks also to my sons, Percy and Pleasant who, along with the rest of the crew, participated in our survey during the process. God bless you all.

My husband, the Venerable Dr. Martin Oguike is my partner in this project. I appreciate all your advice. I thank you for taking time out of your extremely busy schedule to read, make comments and write the foreword to this book. Your love and support are worth more than millions. God bless you immensely.

Above all, the Lord God Almighty, the Father, the Son and the Holy Spirit, Who have enabled me to put these studies into a book; I stand in awe of You. I worship You. May Your love and peace abound for every couple who will read this book and for all families that will receive Your word! Amen!

Foreword

It is a great privilege and blessing to be asked to write a Foreword to this erudite piece of work, *To Have and To Hold*, written by my wife, Dr. Mrs. Ngozi Martin-Oguike. She could have easily asked for a foreword for her book from top-notch marriage counsellors and well-acclaimed biblical scholars or higher-class clerics who will append their big names on the book, to give it more recognition and fame. Reading through the book, I came to realize that it was born out of our 30 years of marriage and 30 years as a pastor's wife and educator with a great deal of experience in family life counseling, and speaking at marriage seminars and workshops for young adults and married couples. This book embodies a wealth of experience and biblical teaching about marriage that will heal troubled marriages or even mend broken ones.

The global rate of divorce and stressful marriages have reached an epidemic proportion even among Christian couples. This long-awaited book will help many married couples *To Have and To Hold* their spouses. The book is simple to read and comes with marriage experiences and examples that we can all identify with. The practical admonition in the book is understandable and easy to follow. The book is replete with lessons for both the man and the woman.

One remarkable feature of this book is that it is not just a panacea for troubled marriages but also an encouragement for couples whose marriages are going in the right direction, to stay on course, 'fixing our eyes on Jesus, the author and perfecter of our faith' (Hebrews 12:2). We will all give an account to Him of how we lived, how we impacted others and how we influenced the next generation.

I consider *To Have and To Hold* a manual for Christian marriage. I recommend it to singles, married couples, pastors, marriage counselors and theological students from diverse Christian denominations and across cultures and races. This is a must read for all that value the Christian institution of marriage.

Martin Oguike, PhD
New Jersey, January 2021

Preface

This book is a product of months of studying Christian marriage vows. It is a practical response to fulfilling our vows in our permissive global community. This started as I was reflecting on my personal experiences and other real life events. I have also taken time to make connections to both traditional and contemporary vows in order to strengthen my own marriage and bear the burdens of others, where needed. Along the line, I was reminded, "...that the race is not to the swift, nor the battle to the strong, neither yet bread to the wise, nor yet riches to men of understanding, nor yet favor to men of skill; but time and chance happeneth to them all" (Ecclesiastes 9:11). As such, I come as a messenger who does not have all the answers. My approach is that of a learner, who involves others in a conversation so we can know together.

I have been comparing traditional with contemporary marriage vows of our time; some in the form of poems, love songs or just verses created by the bride and groom. As interesting as they sound, some of these statements leave you wondering if they are really vows. In a recent wedding we attended, the couple's vows were so poetic that I took interest in some of their declarations. They recalled their walk with each other and exchanged promises. The bride pledged to give her groom beautiful babies. As idealistic as they may be, they failed to capture the strength of a vow. I see some of these proclamations more as fantasy than reality. For instance, to have children is a wish and not a vow. It is a gift of grace and should be stated as such. It is a desire that only God can grant. So, some contemporary vows do not focus on God's Word and His will but on individual desire.

Some of the most amusing 'vows' come from new breed groups by those who play God and make empty vows like, "For better, for better," "for richer, for richer," because they refuse to accept to undergo any form of hardship. Their leaders do not understand the legality of a vow and fail to realize that marriage is a covenant. No wonder the spate of divorce among Christians in recent times! Obviously, people have not studied the entire Bible and are ill-prepared for trials and tribulations, which come to individuals, couples and families in spite of faith and spirituality. Therefore, this book is a reminder that in Christian marriage we pledge to "have and to hold" each other all the days of our lives, whether or not things go well for us. That is the crux of our wedding vows. This message will change any negative mindset and strengthen marriages. It is a call to reveal the best of your spouse and enjoy marriage.

In this study, we need to encourage one another. As part of a wedding congregation, that's what you would promise during a wedding ceremony. Often, when we hear stories of failed relationships and marriages, we are quick to cast blames on another and that does not help anyone. Far too many marriages have ended in regrets and bitterness, which could have been prevented, if we actually knew what to do to help. This is a call to be your brother's keeper.

I weep each time a person goes into marriage on a shaky foundation. More so, when a previously happy marriage begins to crumble due to selfishness and lack of wisdom. In the ministry, we find that more and more distressed marriages are the products of poor decisions due to desperation and prayerlessness. Hence, *To Have and to Hold* is an attempt to reach out to God-fearing couples who want to develop lasting relationships and enjoy marriage as long as both of them shall live. It is a reminder that God is the author of marriage and there is life beyond courtship and the wedding ceremony. Yes, real life events really begin after the dotted lines have been signed. Some will say that the masks are then removed and real faces are revealed. That's why the scenarios in this book are nonfiction occurrences. I have captured a few of the numerous stories that we have heard in recent years. I tremble at how believers are losing their faith due to unhappy and unstable marriages and do hope that this conversation will heal a broken heart and restore failed relationships, marriages and families.

This is a message of hope; a reminder that each one needs to play a part for the success of the bond. Yet, if we have taken the wrong step, there is still hope. We have only one place to go: to the God of reconciliation, the God of love, who can restore all things. He is the one true God, the author of marriage and the one who did his first earthly miracle at the marriage in Cana of Galilee (John 2:11). The one who has left us the Comforter, the Holy Spirit that enables us to pray and to pray aright.

As I reached the last chapter of this book, it became obvious to me that there is still so much to be said and the message is unending. So, if God wills, we shall continue in another study. My prayer is that all who read this book will receive the touch of God that will strengthen their faith and build them up in the holy estate of marriage.

Dr. Ngozi Martin-Oguike

Chapter 1

TRADITIONAL MARRIAGE VOWS

During a wedding ceremony, the celebrant will ask the congregation for the last time if they are in agreement to the marriage. If no one brings up any reason why the couple should not be joined together in holy matrimony, then he will make the following charge:

> *I require and charge you both, here in the presence of God, that if either of you know any reason why you may not be united in marriage lawfully, and in accordance with God's Word, you do now confess it.*
> (Book of Common Prayer 1662)

While everyone is silent, the officiating minister will look the couple in the eye for a response. In most cases, there will be no response. There have been confessions or refusal to go on in very few instances. But this is the last time to speak out. Only the bravest can do so at this point. Many keep quiet even when they are not convinced to go on.

The declaration of consent

The Celebrant says to the woman
N., Will you have this man to be your husband; to live together in the covenant of marriage? Will you love him, comfort him, honor and keep him, in sickness and in

health; and, forsaking all others, be faithful to him as long as you both shall live?

The woman answers
I will.

The celebrant says to the man
N., will you have this woman to be your wife; to live together in the covenant of marriage? Will you love her, comfort her, honor and keep her, in sickness and in health; and, forsaking all others, be faithful to her as long as you both shall live?

The man answers
I will.

Both the man and the woman consciously declare that they will work on their marriage. I suppose that is why we talk about the age of consent. I know that in New Jersey, if you want to marry before the age of 18, parent consent is needed. Most couples reach the age of consent before they take their vows.

The Celebrant then addresses the congregation, saying
Will all of you witnessing these promises do all in your power to uphold these two persons in their marriage?

People
We will.

This places some level of responsibility on the members of the congregation. It is their duty to pray for and uphold the couple and not tear apart the home.

The exchange of vows is the high point of a wedding. The man takes the woman into the holy estate of matrimony, "to love her, comfort her, honor and keep her in sickness and in health, forsaking all others, and keeping only unto her, so long as they both shall live." He must answer in the affirmative, "I will." The vows indicate that the only reason for separation is death. The unresolved question is: who is qualified to preside over separation or divorce?

In continuation, the minister will ask the woman,
> *Will you have this man in the holy state of matrimony, obey him, serve him, love, honor, keep him in sickness and in health, forsaking all others, and keep only unto him, as long as you both shall live?*

And the woman will respond,
> *I will.*

Both the man and the woman do promise to keep their marriage holy, to love, honor and keep each other, and to forsake all others and keep to themselves only. While the man pledges to comfort his wife, the woman vows to obey and serve her husband. After these vows, the two are joined to become one in a declaration as follows:

> *I take thee* ___ *to be my wedded wife. To have and to hold* (to become mine) *from this day forward* (Marriage has a starting point. It doesn't just happen. That's why we celebrate anniversaries). *For better, for worse* (whatever we have to pass through; come what may), *for richer, for poorer* (it doesn't matter if we prosper or suffer lack). *In sickness and in health* (whether I am capable of physically satisfying you or I'm too weak to do

so), *to love and to cherish* (with unconditional love and devotion), *till death us do part* (our union has an expiry time between wedding and death of one of us).

Thereto I plight thee my troth.
The old English words plight and troth were used in the Book of Common Prayer (BCP) 1662. These are strong action words that are defined as:

> *Plight* – to pledge or promise solemnity, one's faith or loyalty

> *Troth* – faithfulness, fidelity, or loyalty; one's word or promise, especially in engaging oneself to marry. (Webster, Merriam Webster Dictionary, 2020)

To plight you my troth means that I promise to be faithful to you. It is an undertaking, a vow that will stand over a period of time. All marriage vows are according to God's holy ordinance. They are sealed with the exchange of rings. A ring or marriage band is a symbol of endless love. As people will describe it, "head over heels in love." So, as round as the ring is, there is no head or tail to the love in a marriage.

With my body I thee worship – I will "worship the ground on which you walk," that is, I will show you total devotion. This is a decision to stand with your spouse in whatever circumstance you two find yourselves.

All my worldly goods, I thee endow – We are together in this. It is teamwork. There is now no difference between your own and my own. We are now one. We have taken up the same name and belong to one another. We share all we have together.

All these promises are made in the name of the Father, the Son and the Holy Spirit. Amen! In the presence of witnesses, many or few. The concluding prayer in the BCP cites Isaac and Rebecca, the Old Testament example of monogamous, faithful marriage in Genesis 24.

At that point, the minster pronounces them man and wife and goes on to bless them. The celebrant prays for them to "so live to the glory of God that you will come to everlasting life." What a declaration! What an act of faith!

Marriage should be the institution that will help us to remain in the faith. That should be the purpose of marriage. Are you marrying someone with whom you hope to keep living for God? Or are you so excited about your spouse that you cannot stop to check if he is ready to go the extra mile with God? Love is completely different from infatuation. When there is love you can wait. When there is lust, someone gets impatient and is afraid of losing the other. True love does not turn into hatred when there is hurt, as in the case of Amnon and Dinah (2 Samuel 13). It is only on the basis of true love that one can make those solemn vows and truly mean them, as in the case of Jacob and Rachael (Genesis 29). Love does not give up and is worth fighting for. Jacob had the worst kind of disappointment in his bid to marry Rachael. After he was deceived, his heart still clung to his true love. So he mustered up courage and served another seven years just to get her. That's love.

What is love? 1 Corinthians 13: 4 – 13

> *Love is patient, love is kind. It does not envy, it does not boast, it is not proud. It does not dishonor others, it is not self-seeking, it is not easily angered, it keeps no record of wrongs. Love does not delight in evil but rejoices with the truth. It always protects, always trusts, always hopes, always perseveres. Love never fails. But where there are prophecies, they will cease; where there are tongues, they will be stilled; where there is knowledge, it will pass away.*
>
> *For we know in part and we prophesy in part, but when completeness comes, what is in part disappears. When I was a child, I talked like a child, I thought like a child, I reasoned like a child. When I became a man, I put the ways of childhood behind me. For now we see only a reflection as in a mirror; then we shall see face to face. Now I know in part; then I shall know fully, even as I am fully known. And now these three remain: faith, hope and love. But the greatest of these is love.*

Marriage vows are so solemn that it is frightening to make such promises to someone who you cannot trust. It is not done with light-heartedness. Love will be shaken and challenged in many ways. You will rethink your decision very often, but can only remain if you laid the right foundation and are ready to please God and uphold your spouse. That foundation is love. True love, based on the Word of God, for "God is love" (1John 4:8).

Chapter 2

A BOND IS MADE

We exchange vows at marriage ceremonies because Christian marriage is a one-track road. Vows demonstrate the gravity of the relationship that starts at the tying of the nuptial knot at the wedding ceremony, as witnesses stand to observe the solemn covenant made. The audience response shows agreement to take responsibility to support the newly wed. The vow is a reminder of your first love, which will wear out as time goes on. Indeed, the vow is a spiritual altar, and stands as where to return to when the going gets tough, and the once burning passion begins to cool down and burn out. That will always occur in real life.

As we reflect on traditional versus modern wedding vows, we clinch while pondering on this avowal; "forsaking all others, keep thee only unto him or her, so long as you both shall live?" and the response: "I will."

"Forsaking" is a word to note here. So, are you really forsaking your friends and family? How possible is it to forsake them? Well, you are changing loyalties. You are becoming one with only one person and are no longer intimately available to all others. To others you have said, No! Hence, you have forsaken, abandoned, jilted, ditched everyone else. As such, you are called to fidelity in your new holy relationship of marriage.

Fidelity: Have you ever wondered why most failed marriages, whether Christian or not, have infidelity in common? Many years back, I visited a newly married couple and met an elderly Christian woman who was advising them. She said frantically to them, "Never, ever give room to infidelity in your marriage, because the day that happens will be the beginning of the end of your happy married life." That was profound, and after three decades, this motherly theory has never once been disproved.

Issues of trust will wreck any relationship, and marriage is not an exception. Do you trust your spouse? Are you trustworthy? Trust begins during courtship. When consummated, "the marriage bed should be undefiled" (Hebrews 13:4).

After a few decades as a believer in Christ, by God's grace and his many mercies, I have learned that Christians are not perfect people living on earth. Believers do err. It is only God that sustains us in the holy estate of marriage. We are not always doing what is right. We are vulnerable and need to humbly accept our weaknesses while leaning on the Lord for sustenance. Thus, we must avoid suspicious behaviors, such as:

1. Lack of trust for others. If you are always skeptical and cannot trust anyone, it may be that you are a hypocrite. This might be real or imaginary; but it would manifest in how we approach each other. For example:

    -   Questioning every move made by your spouse

- Being afraid when your spouse wants to travel on a job-related trip

- Treating your spouse like a minor during meetings with friends

2. Growing distance between the two. This might be obvious or inadvertent; yet it shows in the following ways:

   -Lack of commitment to the relationship

   -Preferring the company of others to that of your spouse

   -Keeping a workaholic lifestyle – suddenly starting to stay late at work

   -A feeling of loneliness while married and staying with your spouse

3. Sin is the killer of matrimony. When one is caught in an act of sin, it becomes difficult to stand together. Sin in marriage is not always adultery. It could also be:

   o Lying to your spouse,

   o Planning to do anything immoral or unethical,

   o Trifling with the opposite gender, and/or

   o Out-rightly committing the sin of adultery

It is very challenging to recover from suspicion in a relationship. But some couples have overcome by the grace and mercy of God. It takes full repentance and forgiveness on both sides. "For if the son of man shall set you free, you are free indeed" (John 8:36).

Theresa had her sister, Ini, visit her home from time to time. She had a great relationship with her husband, Brown. While she was not wary of him, Brown sincerely confessed to her that he had been having a romantic relationship with Ini. Theresa was taken aback. She never imagined that her husband could imagine such a thing. It was unbearable for her. Anger and disgust took the greater part of her. Theresa became bitter and refused to forgive her once beloved husband for a long time. It was in a group counseling session that she discovered that she was not alone in that kind of betrayal. She spoke to a Christian counselor and, together, they identified the real enemy of her marriage, who is Satan. She decided to forgive Brown, who seemed truly repentant. They have forged ahead together ever since. Theresa took back her wedded husband, "to have and to hold."

When there is genuine repentance by your spouse, you will see his or her willingness to rebuild the broken trust. Then you should forgive and restore your relationship through love. How could Theresa be sure Brown would not hurt her again? Supposing he does it again, what can she do?

Seventy times seven is the teaching of Jesus Christ on the importance of forgiveness:

> Then came Peter to him, and said, Lord, how oft shall my brother sin against me, and I forgive him? till seven times? Jesus saith unto him, I say not unto thee, Until seven times: but, Until seventy times seven. (Matthew 18:21-22)

Does this also apply to marriage? As humans, both of you will once in a while offend each other. Forgiveness applies to you and all of us, and not just for your friends or foes but also your own spouse. The act of forgiveness helps us to be faithful to our vows. It brings reconciliation as the avenue for personal renewal. If we understand this teaching, we can love unconditionally.

Chapter 3

NOURISH YOUR MARRIAGE

Have you wondered about the number of previously firebrand brethren who are today enduring their marriages? What about middle-aged believers who are now divorced? Some marriages have become extremely toxic and violent and many are no longer enduring. Most of the time, this happens due to loss of relationship with God, which manifests in broken relationships with people. There is wisdom in quick reconciliation with your spouse so that your marriage is not threatened.

Afam believes his marriage was a mistake. He laments that he knows who he should have married. He has had one failed marriage and the second one is still unhappy; he is trying to cope in order to maintain the ministry. My advice to him was to make the best of where he is. "Be where you're at," as stated in Ebonics. I emphasized the need to be the right person by doing what is right, as stated in Eph. 5:25, 29:

> *Husbands, love your wives, just as Christ also loved the church and gave himself for her...No one ever hated his own flesh, but nourishes and cherishes it, just as the Lord does the church.*

Think about where you started off and how far you have gone. Listen to the Holy Spirit, Who transforms lives, so that you will continue in the love of Christ. "Remember your first love" (Revelations 2:4,5).

How are you nourishing and cherishing your spouse? When you nourish something, it looks good, so you cherish it the more. Marriage is a garden, which flourishes only when you take good care of it. Cultivate and prune your plants and you will be the proud owner of blooming crops and reap a bountiful harvest. That's how it works!

Marriage is a great house. It takes time and resources to build. And that is not all! It is only the beginning of the greater responsibility of maintenance. The larger the building, the more onerous the task of its upkeep. It needs cleaning, refurbishing and patching. The Wiseman says:

"A wise woman builds her own house, but the foolish tears it down with her own hands" (Proverbs 14:1). The same applies to a wise man. What are you doing to your home? Are you building or breaking it down? After you have made your vows, your relationship will continue to thrive if you:

> Resolve to be the best wife or husband you can be
>
> Pray and study the word of God together everyday
>
> Continue to date and hang out together; this should not end because you're now married
>
> Do things together – travel, eat, watch movies, etc.
>
> Treat your spouse specially and not as one of the kids. He or she is your body.
>
> Are not too busy for intimacy. It is like keeping oil on the wheel.

Avoid sleeping in separate rooms. Do not create the loneliness; be open. There is no place for secrecy in marriage.

Allow your spouse to cry on your shoulder and cry along or console him or her rather than blaming or walking away when one of you is vulnerable

Be sincere to each other and do not cover for his or her sin. Rather, point it out, based on the word of God

Do all in love and not to judge. Remember the story of Ananias and Sapphira in Acts 5, the couple that lied to the Holy Spirit. Let's stand for truth in our marriage. Ananias agreed with his wife Sapphira to do what other members of the church are doing. People were selling their property and donating money to the team. Peter was in leadership and he was filled with the Holy Spirit. Barnabas sold his piece of land and donated everything to God. Just as many have donated to purchase lands and build churches in our time. Ananias and Sapphira wanted to do the same. They sold their land and donated money to the church. That was generous of them. Nevertheless, there was a problem: they told the brethren that they gave everything, but they did not. They were lying. Ananias came first and lied to Peter and the other disciples, then Sapphira came forward. She would have lived if only she stood on the truth. She could just have told the simple truth: we sold it for $10,000 and agreed to donate $5,000 to help the group. But no, she did not. They both wanted to appear spiritual and generous by saying, That's all!

Peter asked, "Did you really sell it so much?" Without a blink, she affirmed the lie. If only one of them cautioned the other and said, "No, no, no! I'll not be part of this dishonesty. God is watching us." Their lives would have been saved. This must have been a great lesson to the early church.

Unity and obedience in marriage does not mean that you submit to disobey God. Some of us have previously been intimidated to say 'Yes' when we knew that the other person was not fully honest. We must help save each other and our family by standing on the truth.

Figure 1: The Marriage Chart

God must be the center of your marriage and family life (Figure 1). With Him at the center, you can never deviate from the goal. God fights your battle and protects you from the enemies of your marriage. Whenever distractions come, you can always look unto God who is the core of your marriage. He is able to keep what He began.

When the husband or wife is being distracted from the marriage, there are signs like: avoiding praying together, being easily irritable, and avoiding simple conversation. It is time to consciously work to get back attention and commitment. Don't be prideful and act as if you don't care. Be reasonable and prayerfully restore your relationship. Not even our children should separate us from loving and caring for each other. If confronted with growing distance in your relationship, you have to address it with a determination to:

Forgive each other no matter what - *and forgive us our sins, as we have forgiven those who sin against us -* (Matthew 6:12)

Respect each other even in the face of hunger and poverty, knowing that no condition is permanent - *However, each one of you also must love his wife as he loves himself, and the wife must respect her husband -* (Ephesians 5:33)

Get reconciled when you discover that you have wronged one another; continue to walk together - *But if we walk in the light, as he is in the light, we have fellowship with one another, and the blood of Jesus, his Son, purifies us from all sin. If we claim to be without sin, we deceive ourselves and the truth is not in us. If we confess our sins, he is faithful and just and will forgive us our sins and purify us from all unrighteousness.* (1John 1:7-9)

Do not nag your spouse with the mistakes of the past - *It is better to dwell in the corner of the housetop than with a brawling woman and in a wide house.* (Proverbs 25:24)

Build your own house with wisdom - *The wise woman builds her house, but with her own hands the foolish one tears hers down.* (Proverbs 14:1)

Like a well-built house, marriage is for keeps and it takes work and resources to maintain. When a house is well-built, decorated with flowers in a well-nurtured garden, the members of the family continue to enjoy life together. What a blessing to have a home that is safe and stable! Even when your family is threatened, the couple will stay together and not move apart. Rather than fight each other, they hold hands and together they look ahead.

Nagging breaks down any relationship. It is very irritating and is a result of faultfinding. It comes from a perfectionist point of view; from one who thinks he or she is always right and cannot tolerate wrong. Real life experiences show that it is most uncomfortable to live with a perfect man or woman. Right from the elementary school, they are quarrelsome, and if they happen to grow with the same attitude, they never have one friend for a long time. As young adults, they get into other people's businesses and cannot live peacefully with a roommate. On the long run, they are likely to weary anyone who happens to take them into their bosom.

Christ changes characters. It is called transformation. Christlikeness is important in marriage. A humble person will not fight over everything: money, food, fashion, party or leadership. Accommodating results in joyous marriage, which is free of nagging, malice and fighting. When matters arise, they are able to discuss in love, not insisting on being right. Nagging does not bear good fruit; rather, "the fruit of the Spirit is love, joy, peace, longsuffering, gentleness, goodness, faith, meekness, temperance: against such there is no law" (Galatians 5:222,23).

Chapter 4

TILL DEATH US DO PART

Marriage is a mystery that has been compared to the relationship between Christ and His church:

Wives, submit yourselves to your own husbands as you do to the Lord. For the husband is the head of the wife as Christ is the head of the church, his body, of which he is the Savior. Now as the church submits to Christ, so also wives should submit to their husbands in everything. Husbands, love your wives, just as Christ loved the church and gave himself up for her to make her holy, cleansing her by the washing with water through the word, and to present her to himself as a radiant church, without stain or wrinkle or any other blemish, but holy and blameless. In this same way, husbands ought to love their wives as their own bodies. He who loves his wife loves himself. After all, no one ever hated their own body, but they feed and care for their body, just as Christ does the church — for we are members of his body. For this reason a man will leave his father and mother and be united to his wife, and the two will become one flesh. This is a profound mystery — but I am talking about Christ and the church. However, each one of you also must love his wife as he loves himself, and the wife must respect her husband. (Ephesians 5:22 – 33)

The mystery of merging two persons into one is only replicative of the love of the Trinity; three persons, one God. Marriage is actually for Christians. It is a divine covenant for those whose love is from God. That statement has continued to resonate with me throughout my adult life. Yes, it will take a more rigorous commitment for two persons to live together come what may. Jesus must be at the center of your lives. He reveals His purpose for every marriage. Each matrimonial relationship must have a vision which answers the essential question: what is the purpose of your marriage?

The reasons for marriage could be summarized as: for companionship, to avoid adultery, and for procreation.

1. Companionship
And the Lord God said, It is not good that the man should be alone; I will make him an help meet for him (Genesis 2:18).

Companionship is the first and most important reason why God created matrimony when he made a woman. Therefore, the man is incomplete without the woman. When Adam saw Eve, he was happy and felt complete. *The man said, "This is now bone of my bones and flesh of my flesh; she shall be called 'woman,' for she was taken out of man* (Genesis 2:23).

When you have a companion, you are strengthened because, *Iron sharpeneth iron; so a man sharpeneth the countenance of his friend* (Proverbs 27:17). Communion with each other brings forth spiritual edification, because *when we fellowship with one another, the blood of Jesus cleanses us from all sins* (1John 1:7).

From the beginning, God understood that the man needed someone else to complement him, someone to care for and to care about him. Unfortunately, Eve listened to the deceiver, ate the forbidden fruit and gave it to her husband, Adam, who also ate. By their joint decision, therefore, they disobeyed God. Supposing Adam took that decision to eat the fruit alone and was driven out by God, what could have happened to him? Nonetheless with Eve, they were able to survive and procreate.

Being the Right Person for Each Other

A lot of people believe that there is just one particular person for each of us. That person is referred to as a life partner or one's *better half.* They literally interpret "bone of my bone and flesh of my flesh" (Genesis 2:23) to mean that you have to find and marry the one right man or woman made for you.

If you fail to find your *bone and flesh,* your future is ruined. In the worldly language, they speak about incompatibility just like a part of a Peugeot vehicle is incompatible with a part of Toyota. As such, the thought of missing your correct rib is dreadful.

In cultures of the past, in which people like Abraham and David married multiple women, I wonder how compatible these women were with them. I know that people do fall head over heels in love with the person that complements them the most; but sometimes, marriages are arranged and they still work out. At other times, marriages come as direct results of revelation or answered prayers and they work out. There have been some spiritually discerned marriages that did not work out in practice.

For those who regret their marriages and wish to turn back the hand of the clock, I have a simple response. Work diligently to make where you are the best it can be. *As you make your bed, so you'll lie on it* is an old saying. You should be ashamed to live in a messed up house and blame someone else for the clutter. It is your duty to build up your relationship and make it work. There are far too few relationships that are made up of demons and not humans. People will usually resolve issues if they have the platform to do so, unlike beasts who fight and hurt themselves. Most of the time, due to pride and distractions, we allow our mistakes to define the rest of our lives. Our joy comes from simply remembering to be there for each other, which is the first reason why God made marriage: companionship. Be a loving and devoted companion. Be passionate and available to your spouse.

2. For Procreation

When the Lord created man and woman, he instructed them to *Be fruitful and multiply; fill the earth and subdue it; have dominion over the fish of the sea, over the birds of the air, and over every living thing that moves on the earth* (Genesis 1:28).

Adam and Eve remained together and gave birth to their sons, Cain and Abel. Fruitfulness is fundamental to God's creation. God wants the extension of His kingdom. When people wanted to remain in the same vicinity, they started building a tower so that all mankind could stay together and not scatter around the earth. But God came among them and confused their language at the *Tower of Babel* (Genesis 11:1-9), leading to the beginning of world languages.

That shows that God wants us to replenish the earth. He hates a nation that kills her own young. The call is to us all to repent from abortion and child molestation; children must be left to grow and thrive. Replenishing the earth is uppermost in God's mind as we continue to bear fruit. The child belongs to everyone and should be nurtured to greatness.

Fruitfulness means that we should ...*go and bear fruit, and that your fruit should remain, that whatever you ask the Father in My name He may give you* (John 15:16). In marriage, we replicate ourselves in our children. What great joy we feel to see our children giving their lives to Christ and standing in the faith! Even much more when they get into the ministry and begin to bear fruit both physically and spiritually.

Procreation does not mean that everyone must have biological children. However, no state, community or individual should control how many children each citizen can have. We are here to take care of the next generation and not to kill them off. Doctors and caregivers must bear that in mind.

Granted, some have had extenuating circumstances for which pregnancies may have been terminated before term. It calls for repentance and renewal. Faith and faithfulness to God is the only way forward. The worst thing the enemy does is to make doctrines out of sin. If you sin, please repent and do nothing to justify evil. Be humble enough to acknowledge sin as sin, and do not return to iniquity.

Jay and Ogo's story calls to mind one of the challenges of the married life. It shows how the choices we make can make or mar our future and reveals God's mercies upon mankind. Ogo got married to her best friend, Jay. They were thrilled to begin to have their own children, who came within their first year of marriage. It was a very difficult pregnancy that almost cost Ogo's life. She emerged from it grateful to God for life restored. She began to recover from the stress as she nursed her baby and returned to work. However, within five months, she was pregnant again and began to bleed in-between. From the ultrasound, they found that the fetus was not properly placed in the womb (I will avoid the use of medical terms here). Long story short, Jay, who was petrified, took her to her gynecologist and, after back and forth drills, the fetus was terminated.

After the experience, Ogo became troubled and could not get over it. She went through the procedure of abortion and suffered a nervous breakdown. She was sad and lonely and her life was no longer the same. Her faith was fractured and she started to experience loneliness and fear for the first time as a believer. When Ogo went to see a minister, they discussed her situation and the pastor realized her deep repentance and contriteness of spirit. He told her that God has forgiven her, because he is God of mercy who searches the reins and the heart. Then he added, "Now your task is to forgive yourself." This took her so many years to do. Ogo testified that she has forgiven herself, although the aftereffect of her vulnerability kept her humble as a believer. She has determined never again to terminate a pregnancy or advise anyone to do so for any reason.

Ogo became angry and resentful and blamed her husband and doctor for suggesting the termination of her pregnancy and for carrying it out. She felt that Jay was not there for her during her most trying moment. She was frustrated, lost weight and began to complain about her marriage. She went through a spate of guilt until she learned to accept responsibility for her decision and spent time seeking God's face and accepting her vulnerability. She now understood that she didn't need to pass the blame as Eve did. Rather, she decided never to take a decision outside of the will and command of God.

When fear comes into your life, you are the only one who will take the decision to conquer it by faith. If you chose to yield to fear, neither your spouse nor the doctor can have the last say but you. Your decision must be based on the word of God. Ogo should have said, "No, I will have my baby no matter what!" She did not stand up to her faith, so she suffered and regretted her inaction. Nevertheless, she did not turn away from the Lord. There was no other place to go. The Lord remained her anchor.

Many years after, Ogo still lives happily with Jay and together they have grown to take stands on spiritual and ethical issues as they continue to live for God as a couple. Some of the steps she took were praying, realizing that she sinned and that it was sin that made her lose her peace. Then she confessed to God and to a minister of God, who prayed for her and counseled her. Ogo fasted and prayed, and studied the word of God on the issue at stake. Finally, she learned to forgive herself. Today, she is ministering life and has not backslidden from the Way. A few years after Ogo's experience, her friend, Ekene, had the same medical problem, Ogo became her main support. They prayed together and God gave them a miracle. Ekene gave birth successfully despite their initial fear. She has continued to be a champion for women going through similar issues.

When biological children come, we are custodians; our major role is to pray for and nurture them after Christ. Our aim should be to bring them to become believers who will stay strong in the Lord. As parents, our first call is to *Train up the child in the way he should go and when he is old he will not depart from it* (Proverbs 22:6). *Children are a heritage of the Lord and a reward* (Psalm 127). We must teach them the word of God (Deuteronomy 11:19). Their purpose is to continue God's plan on earth, replenishing the earth. Nevertheless, everyone must learn that each person shall stand at the judgement alone. You must search yourself and receive power to prevail.

3. To Avoid Adultery

Lust is an ongoing sin that every believer must flee: *Flee also youthful lusts: but follow righteousness, faith, charity, peace, with them that call on the Lord out of a pure heart* (2Timothy 2:22). Lust is dangerous because it leads to adultery, if uncurbed. The seventh commandment says, "Thou shall not commit adultery" (Exodus 20:14).

Jesus further expounds it, *But I say to you that whoever looks at a woman to lust for her has already committed adultery with her in his heart* (Matthew 5:28). This also relates to the woman who lusts after a man.

The human mind is an engine that gathers rust and stains from the environment. Some do isolate themselves from the influence of corrosive elements, but all need extra power to keep from being tarnished. Oil is needed to keep the machine and protect it from dust and corrosion. When the word of God comes with anointing of the Holy Spirit, it produces the anointing oil for protecting the mind from worldly influence and corruption. Lust comes with the desires of the flesh and is fueled by the pressure from all around. Lust after money, lust after fashion and lust after the works of the flesh all lead to adultery and fornication. These alter peaceful family life and joyous living. Lust comes as an internal conflict that must be fought individually through deep relationship with God in all sincerity. By walking in obedience to God, we conquer lust. You should be ready to put away carnal ways of thinking and living, for *to be carnally minded is death; but to be spiritually minded is life and peace* (Romans 8:6).

Do you love God? Then, *flee youthful lust and pursue righteousness, faith, love and peace, along with those who call on the Lord out of a pure heart* (2 Timothy 2:22). God hates uncleanness. So when you catch yourself dwelling in lust, you have to return to the Lord and pray for cleansing. Then pursue righteousness. Study and meditate on the word of God.

> *Whatsoever things are true, whatsoever things are honest, whatsoever things are just, whatsoever things are pure, whatsoever things are lovely, whatsoever things are of*

good report; if there be any virtue, and if there be any praise, think on these things (Philippians 4:8).

You are made up of the quality of your thought. Trying to prove that certain sins do not matter is deceitful and will lead to a hardening of the heart. Believers must walk sincerely with God and seek His righteousness, and not be comfortable with sin; else, their hearts will be hardened by sin. *And even as they did not like to retain God in their knowledge, God gave them over to a debased mind, to do those things which are not fitting* (Romans 1:28).

The question is: does youthful lust stop at youth or continue after marriage and up to an older age? Well, the fight is with the flesh and, as long as we are in the flesh, the constant fight continues in the mind. It is an internal conflict that only the Holy Spirit can help resolve. However, the marriage mindset helps a lot, because when you are married you know you are committed and have pledged to be faithful to your spouse. An effective, God-centered courtship helps focus the desire on one another. The process of marriage counseling, seminars and different activities for engaged couples help with transitioning into the marriage mindset. However, some people get married and continue to hang out with singles and find it difficult to build their new relationship. If one does not accept the reality and purpose of marriage, he or she will be like Aga, who had to learn it the hard way.

While a student on campus, Aga was there for all the brethren. He went wherever he wanted, came back whenever he liked and attended whatever classes he was interested in. It actually took him seven years to complete his four-year degree and he couldn't wait to graduate and get married. The wedding was over, but the exuberance did not wear out. Aga remained the same vivacious brother gallivanting all over the place and making things happen. He was a preferred preacher and resource person at many campus groups and was often at one college or the other sharing the word! His wife, Ann sometimes went along with him. Gradually, she stopped going because she couldn't keep up with the late nights and long discussions after services, in which she was often ignored by people who were only interested in talking to her husband. Shortly after, it became obvious to her that she had rushed into marriage.

Aga thought he could have done better a celibate. He found himself being closer to members of his ministry team than to his wife and child. He was not even present in the life of his son. Inadvertently, he neglected his family. One day, after a long week away, he returned and discovered that his wife had moved out. She left their son with his parents and traveled abroad. That was the end of his marriage and a blow to his ministry. Many years have passed and Aga is still struggling to pick up the broken pieces of his life. If these two had been humble enough to seek help, their future together would have been secured. But they were too proud to realize that they needed help. Yet, it is not too late for them to swallow their pride and return to each other. Each one must be ready to accommodate the other.

In a recent discussion with this "powerful" brother, I found that it has dawned on him that he had taken so much for granted in his failed marriage. He confessed that he acted selfishly and never thought of how his actions affected his immediate family. Yet, he was unsure of how he would move ahead as he made effort to restore his relationship with his wedded wife. Meanwhile, Ann thought she had enough and could not trust him to know how to make a home. The conversation has resumed and, with prayers and utmost humility, it is bound to be successful. Marriage is companionship, a safe haven from lust. But it can only work if the two are there to support each other.

Chapter 5

BEING THE RIGHT PERSON

It is depressing to think that you must have married the wrong person. That is truly being in jail by choice. However, if you believe the word of God and accept that ...*all things work together for good to them that love God, to them who are called according to His purpose* (Romans 8:28), you can know by faith that all will be well. When I hear brethren constantly express regrets over seemingly marriage mistakes, I'm quick to remind them that the issue is not **finding** the right person but **being** the right person; that is a choice and a personal determination.

To become a Christian, you get born again by deliberately choosing to accept Jesus Christ into your life and living in obedience to God's word. It is known as repentance, a turnaround; it is a choice. God does not force us to come to him. Some choose to live by double standards, while others fully surrender. It is purposeful. Remember, the man, Jairus who was bent on getting healing for his daughter: he went for it and got it! (Matthew 5:21-43). The importunate widow could not be stopped; she kept returning until she received her request (Luke 18:1-8); even blind Bartimaeus resisted all encumbrances in order to receive his healing (Mark 10:46-52). In the same way, it takes effort to stay married. In your scale of preference, your marriage should be next to your relationship with God. Think of the woman who touched the hem of Jesus' garment in Matthew 9:20-22. She could not be stopped, but said, "if only I can touch the hem of his garments, I will be whole." She pressed on until she did and her faith made her whole.

If you commit it into the hands of God and ask for grace to be the right person from beginning to the end, your marriage will not only survive; it will thrive. You must walk in obedience. Unlike Peter, who left his calling to return to fishing, you should endeavor to remain in your calling within your marital home:

> *Now to the married I command, yet not I but the Lord: A wife is not to depart from her husband. But even if she does depart, let her remain unmarried or be reconciled to her husband. And a husband is not to divorce his wife.* (1Corinthians 7:10,11)

Do not abandon your family responsibility. Simon, son of Jonas, was far gone back to the world when Jesus met him again (John 21:15-19). The Master was not going to give up on his nurtured disciple. He reinstated Peter in verse 18, "Follow me...." We really need to follow Him to fulfill our calling. Here, I am reflecting on the question that Jesus asked Peter: "Do you love me?" and Jesus' responses, especially, "Tend my sheep".

To tend means to regularly and frequently behave in a particular way or have a certain characteristic; be inclined; apt, disposed to, prone to, liable; have or show a tendency; be likely; or have a propensity to do something. The Merriam Webster dictionary defines it as:

> To exhibit an inclination or tendency. Tends to be optimistic
>
> To move, direct, or develop one's course in a particular direction.

We must tend our marriages and families towards God, thereby leading them to follow the right path.

After the death and resurrection of Jesus Christ, Peter and other disciples went back to fishing. Jesus reappeared to them and there performed another stupendous miracle of catching fish (John 21). The disciples recognized the Lord (v. 7). It was a great revelation as their eyes opened to realize that it was the Master at it again. This was in line with their past experience: whenever the Lord entered, there were miracles following. Jesus was the director of supernatural occurrences. The miracle of that day was a confirmation of the power of resurrection working among them. Imagine that the net did not break (v. 11). Jesus then called on Peter:

> "Simon … do you love me more than these…? Feed my lambs" (v.15)
>
> "Simon,…do you love Me?… Tend my sheep" (v.16)
>
> "Simon…do you love me?…Feed my sheep" (v.17)

Jesus went on to address Peter:

When you were younger, you girded yourself and walked where you wished. But when you are old you will stretch out your hands and another will gird you and carry you where you do not wish. Follow me. (John 21:19)

We are enjoined to love fully so we can follow completely. It's very difficult to follow a person you do not love and trust. This is a word for those going into courtship. You have to understand and trust His leading so you will rely fully on Him. He says, "Follow me. I will make you fishers of men" (Matthew 4:19).

What did Jesus mean by "Tend My Sheep"? Other key verbs that describe 'tend' are: attend, serve, listen to, await, watch over, take charge of (as a caretaker), oversee, cultivate, mind, and manage. The Latin word, *tendere* means to extend outwards, stretch, spread, and spread out. So, "tend my sheep" is a grave command. It has to be a labor of love. Marriage is a covenant of love. If you love me, tend my sheep. That means, don't just say you love me, do something to show it. Step up to the plate, obey my command, act on it, be like me.

Do you remember that child who wants to be like you? It might be your daughter or sister or younger friend, coworker or student who adores you. Point them first to Jesus. He says, "Follow me." Each of us is called to a vocation. Peter was called to be an apostle. He was commissioned to be a "fisher of men" (Matthew 4:19). When so many fish or men were caught, Jesus asked him to "tend" them: Support them, equip them with the word and make them fishers of men also.

Recently, I've been asking the question: where is the true church? The nucleus of the church is in our homes. It is made up of our marriages, families and children. If you first love the Lord, you will be the right person for your spouse.

You are being called to tend the sheep in your enclave. Do not let the sheep run free range. They are not chicken or wolves. Let us tend them, and bring them close. Don't lose them. Seek them. Show them a good example for living. Work together in humility and build your home to the glory of God.

The revival is coming. Many prophets are proclaiming the new dawn. It will begin with ministers recognizing their gifts and calling and using them to glorify God and edify the church. It will come with awakening of the gifts and power in the body of Christ. That's where it begins: feed your family, tend your marriage, tend your relationship. Marriage is a covenant, a call from God; walk in obedience, be faithful. Do not look around and get distracted; rather, feed the Lord's sheep. Nourish the family under your care. Allow the love of God to reign in your marriage by being the right person to your spouse. Make your contributions to the welfare and success of all. You are called by the Lord Jesus to "tend my sheep!"

Building a marriage and keeping it flourishing requires us to "be separate!" (2 Cor. 6:17) and "holy, for I am holy" (1Peter 1:16); being sanctified to the Lord. There is a time to be separated for prayer and fasting, self-searching, quietness and meditation on the word.

There is a time to just wait on the Lord; not as a routine or religious duty, but because you need to purposely separate yourself (spirit, soul and body) to focus on the Lord, who alone can cleanse and sanctify you for His greater use. We are in a world that is filled with corrupt practices. Everywhere is polluted and people do not even realize it because they can no longer spot the difference between the profane and the divine. This obscurity is so prevalent that even in Christian marriage, we sometimes forget the sacred vow we took before God and His people. In so doing, so many have shipwrecked their homes. Many run into the risk of putting their spouses last in the scheme of things, thus taking their own bodies for granted, which is a recipe for crisis.

Jesus has told us that the "two shall be one" (Mark 10:8). So, you love and nourish your body as a responsibility. When you treat your husband or wife poorly, you are no longer nourishing your body but separating from it. You are putting part of your body asunder. The call is to build up and not break down what God has joined together. We vowed to be together in holy matrimony till death us do part. It is a worrisome position to be helping lawfully wedded couples to separate or dissolve their union. Even more dreadful is to be involved in remarriage for people whose ex-spouses are still living. My heart bleeds to see the extent to which the church has progressed into divorce and separation matters, with little or no just cause.

When the disciples wanted to know what Jesus thought about divorce, He told them, "because of your hardness of heart, Moses permitted you to give a certificate of divorce, but it was not so from the beginning" (Matthew 19:8).

In the beginning, God meant for marriage to be a final state. He has not changed his perfect will. His perfect will is that we go into marriage cautiously and advisedly so that we do not regret and desire to turn back. However, some believers have made mistakes and have decided they can no longer continue. Some have hardly been joined together when they realized that they have been duped or caged in by a criminal-minded fellow, whose intentions are nothing but dubious. So, why didn't they know before the joining? Well, due to pretense before marriage some only begin to see clearly soon after wedding. At that point, the knot has been tied — notwithstanding, many do decide to live with that. As troubling as it is, that's what a vow does to a person.

Meanwhile, that's why prayerful courtship is beneficial. Naka does not profess to be a Christian. She has refused to go to the altar to wed the father of her child, because she doesn't want the finality of marriage; yet they have been together for ten years. She would jokingly say, "If it's not broken, don't try to fix it." Despite my disapproval, she believes marriage is an overrated ceremony. I'm sure you know people like her. Nevertheless, we know that God made marriage for some reasons.

Marriage is not an open relationship. He made them male and female and declared them man and woman for companionship, fellowship and procreation. If marriage is not providing any or all of these, is it an unsuccessful union? No! It rather means that couples must work together and depend on God for the future of their home.

Funny enough, some marriages become illegal before they are contracted. What does that mean? Before the exchange of vows, the minister will ask:

> *If either of you know any impediment, why you may not be lawfully joined together in matrimony, ye do now confess it. For be ye well assured that so many as are coupled together otherwise than God's word doth allow are not joined together by God; neither is their matrimony lawful.*

I've read this declaration over and over again and I saw why Christian marriage is different. It's not the same as the fair weather relationship that Naka has been in for ten years. It's a well-thought out, God-founded institution of its own, which is established after the searching of hearts and intentions. It is a one-man, one-woman relationship that only ends at the death of one or both of them. Is that your understanding of Christian marriage? If so, are you carefully tending and nurturing your relationship? If not, then you may be in something other than Christian marriage. It doesn't depend on the venue of the ceremony. It could be done on your porch, a park, a church or a waterfront. Yes, anywhere before the presence of God! Marriage is a spiritual covenant.

In the course of marriage preparation and counseling, the bride and groom are taught the meaning and implications of marriage, which parents should have taught them by exemplary living. They will now do background checks to rule out incestuous relationship and any other biological impediments. At the point of wedding, truth must have been told. Prior to approaching the altar, each must confess to the other regarding their past life. Serious and unserious past relationships must have been discussed and, if there were children before marriage, the circumstances must be known to both spouses. Why then will the minister still be asking for confessions on the day of solemnization of holy matrimony?

It is important to keep asking and to clear all doubts until the deed is done. It is also of much importance to ask publicly for general records, so the pastor will never be accused of wedding anyone illegally. Anglican and key protestant traditions have publications of banns of marriage. The public is informed of intending marriages so they can report any known obstacle. The banns are read on three consecutive Sundays before the wedding ceremony. Nevertheless, the question is still asked at the wedding event. Of course, some intended marriages have been discontinued at the point of wedding. Brides and grooms have changed their minds or someone had come up with accusations that led to the end of a wedding, up till the last hour.

I think the church fathers had divine wisdom because even in this 21st century, I have heard of a married man who got engaged to a lady in another country, pretending never to have been married. He made the woman, who was desperate to get married, to spend her money for a society wedding, officiated by high church clerics and celebrated with pomp and pageantry. After that, she started to process immigration papers for him to join her.

The wedding ended, and everyone else returned home; papers were now being processed. Unfortunately for him, the cat was let out of the bag. His new wife had a visit from his village. Things fell apart when the visitor divulged the secret of his double marriage. As his dishonesty was revealed, the angry new wife pulled the plug to all immigration plans. He had the dubious intention of leaving the poor lady immediately after he obtained his position in the newfound country. Tales are unending about how people deceive others into marriage with the intention of conning them. Both men and women have been victims of such unlawful relationships.

A Christian's intention ought to be pure. Marriage requires self-searching and openness. If you have a plan B before your marriage, you also need to confess it to/ discuss it with your spouse. If you want God to uphold your new home, then you have to be in a legal marriage. You must not be a gold digger whose only intent is gain. If you are keeping secrets that, when revealed, will destroy your marriage, you are not ready for marriage. Your marriage is illegal even before it is contracted.

One reality story is that of Stella and Andy, who came together to the US along with their children. They were in a lot of stress. As Stella went to school, Andy worked several long shifts to support his family. Then Stella graduated and started working and their hardship began to lighten. One day, Stella was returning from work and was involved in a car accident. Andy was terrified and ran around to help her. She had minor injuries and their car was totally destroyed. Thankfully, the other driver was at fault and she recovered from her wounds and was discharged from hospital. Andy pressed charges along with their insurance. When all was completed, they were awarded a two million-dollar compensation. As soon as Stella received the check, she moved it into her personal account, took her children and moved out of the house before her husband returned from his last shift of the day.

When Andy returned home, he was still in high spirits; in excitement, he rushed in to celebrate their victory with his family. As he entered their apartment, he was struck by the empty room; the wardrobes were wide ajar. Stella had won a jackpot and decided to relocate and leave her "loser" husband behind. Another example of a foolish woman who believed that the end justifies the means and has no conscience at all.

After several years, Andy still walks about looking bewildered. He still cannot believe he had been tricked by a woman he devoted his life to. This is an illegal marriage, where one partner is there for monetary gains. These are the ones that say, "for better, for better; for richer, for richer." They reject sickness and always vow to be there when the spouse is in good health. In the meantime, they are there for their children and cannot stand the man that married them. That's why the officiant has to counsel a couple before marriage. You must search yourselves to ascertain that you are the right person in your marriage.

Enduring the Matrimonial Stress

Nneka, who was formerly married to Okedi, told me that during their pre-marriage counseling, the pastor had asked her fiancé if he loved her and he said he did not. The pastor told her what he said and asked her to make a last minute decision. She was bitter, but decided to go ahead and wed him. What was her intention for marrying someone who clearly did not love her? Did she make the right decision? Or did she think things would change? That marriage started on a loveless footing and did not endure the stress test at all.

...for better for worse, for richer for poorer; in sickness and in health, to love and to cherish...

You must be madly in love to be able to withstand the battle that lies ahead.

When the going moves from better to worse, richer to poorer and good health begins to dwindle, how steadfast will you be? It is a beautiful sight to see a couple after 50 years of marriage, still holding hands, making jokes and teasing each another as they walk along on their God-chosen path. When we see young couples who soon become cantankerous to each other, we wonder if they chose to follow the few negative examples around them. I just think the majority of marriages follow the pledge, "for better, for worse." I have seen far too many couples living together successfully that I will subscribe to marriage any time. It is the best place to be. However, coming into it with wrong intentions always yield wrong results. For, as you make your bed, so you will lie on it.

Onome always wanted a good life for herself. When she got married to Dankwa, it was because she wanted to relocate with him to Canada. She had always dreamed of traveling abroad and was ready for a quick wedding. Onome was so glad to be married off. Within a couple of months, they left for Canada to start life as husband and wife. When Dankwa was prosperous, Onome enjoyed with him; each time they had financial challenges, she complained and blamed herself for rushing into marriage with him, openly chiding herself for allowing him to deceive her into marriage. They had a seemingly stable relationship. Dankwa took her to many places and provided for her and their children. One day, he lost his job, and that was it! Onome became belligerent and began to join his enemies to fight him. In the midst of that, Dankwa fell ill and died. Then she realized her folly; but it was too late.

It is always good to know that tough times come and go. All we need is to be the support our families need at difficult times. However, most people play the blame game and are too quick to claim to be in the right. That's why Onome lives in regret up till today. She tells stories of great times she had with her husband; nevertheless, their close associates know that she did not treat him well at the time of his vulnerability. She was not even there for him when he was sick, because her marriage was for better and not for worse.

At whatever stage of marriage you are right now, decide to be the right person for your spouse. Love each other and seek to do all within your power to enjoy life together. Marriage is the party that takes place even in the midst of stress, hardship and trouble. Are you the right person for the jamboree? Yes, it is "for better, for worse."

Chapter 6

CHASING SHADOWS

It's so hilarious to hear what causes problems in marriages. Surprisingly, minor issues degenerate into real crises and do not stop until families are destroyed. When you stop to compare the stories you hear to your regular experience, you can only laugh. After all, you are still happily married. So, why are people quarreling and killing each other? It appears people value things more than life. They cannot let go being taken for granted. Others take matters so seriously, and so on and so forth.

Recently, a couple quarreled and eventually divorced because of tax refund from the government. If only they were in a country where there is no tax refund system, maybe they would still be married and would have spared their children the mental stress they've undergone as their parents fought unendingly.

In another case, Shide and Kyle fought because Kyle wanted to travel out of the country alone, every year. At one point, Shide started to challenge him; but he still travelled overseas. When he came back, Shide had bought him out of their house. She gave him his part of the money and booted him out. Case closed! Story ended!

Why can't one give in for the sake of peace? Many people believe that when a marriage works, it is because the relationship is made in heaven. As such, the couple do not need to work on their relationship. It just happens. Yet, experience tells us that this is far from the truth. As some would say, 'marriage is give and take.' In my native Igbo language, the husband is referred to as 'patience.' The Igbo word for husband is a syllable of the word 'patience'. Hence, marriage is said to be wrought in perseverance and understanding.

When matrimony thrives, it must have gone through some challenges. It takes two persons with the mind of God to stay dedicated. Your marriage succeeds when you: accept your faults, apologize to each other, love unconditionally, are angry but not sin, go the extra mile to help, serve without complaining, are looking out for your spouse, are sometimes considered a fool for Christ's sake, refuse to quarrel and nag, and are frugal with your family resources.

Marriages flourish when each one fulfils his or her duty towards the other. Paul's in-depth teaching on marriage outlines expectations and responsibilities within the Christian marriage.

Wives submit

Paul teaches the church of God, saying:

> *Wives, submit yourselves unto your own husbands, as unto the Lord. For the husband is the head of the wife, even as Christ is the head of the church and He is the Savior of the body. Therefore, as the church is subject unto Christ, so let the wives be to their own husband in everything.* (Ephesians 5:22-24)

The keywords are submission, reverence, unto the Lord. The analogy of the church and Christ's relationship is so deep, as in, "wives, submit yourselves unto your own husbands, as it is fit in the Lord" (Colossians 3:18). The depth of submission portrays the extent of love, because we submit to Christ who loves us unconditionally; hence, love is the bedrock of marriage.

Meanwhile, Peter instructs wives, "Ye wives, be in subjection to your own husbands, that if any obey not the word, they also may without the word be won by the conversation of the wife ..." (1 Peter3:1). That means that a wife's way of life can win her husband to Christ. How powerful and profound! This gives us the spiritual strength to encourage each other and make the weak strong and the unbelieving to receive faith. The husband or wife's faith is able to break the other and win them over to Christ. True faith has a sanctifying effect on marriage.

A wife should be in subjection and live in obedience not just in word. Her adornment should reflect modesty and she should have a meek and quiet spirit. With this instruction, we must consider the times we are in and understand the vows we took. Nevertheless, the three descriptions of the godly wife: subjection, obedience and modesty tell about humility and not servitude and bondage.

I often wonder why the woman had to be reminded to be subject and obedient. Paul did remind the women in the church that it was Eve that was deceived and not Adam. That's food for thought. He probably implied that if the woman was not under authority, she would make many more mistakes. As we study these scriptures, we must be careful to keep them in historical and cultural perspectives while not forgetting that God is the author of order. I just think that God organized the family with the protection of all in mind. Wives must submit to their own husbands. Reverence and respect are acts of love.

Husbands, love your wives

Some husbands have taken liberty to subjugate their wives, citing those passages of scriptures. They forget the call to "love your wives" "honor your wife" and their vow to protect her. Marriage is certainly not a jail sentence as many view it. Rather, it is a partnership where mutual respect is paramount. You cannot maltreat your wife because you were made the head of the house. It is not a sin for her to have accepted to marry you. Many wives have lost far too much for anyone to subjugate them for the rest of their lives. They have left their family names and careers to start afresh. They need to be honored and that is what the scriptures command. People just pick and choose what they want to emphasize. My emphasis is to honor her!

Eddy had an arranged marriage with Paulina. He travelled to Nigeria to contract the marriage and celebrate the wedding. The two got married and he returned to his base abroad. After a couple of years, he was able to bring her over to live with him in the US. Meanwhile, he never failed to remind her that he was spending too much on her. Whenever she asked for money, he explained to her how hard it is to make money in this part of the world. She was afraid to ask for anything; but she was focused on her studies and did not want to agitate him. Eventually, Paulina got her certification and license to work and bagged a well-paid job in the city. It took a few months for the table to turn and the bitterness of all the insults she endured to wreck their seemingly stable marriage.

Mutual respect is important in all circumstances, no matter who is the breadwinner. At least, we know that no condition is permanent. Jesus respected everyone, including women and children. The disregard of a woman based on her gender is utter disregard for the word of God that says, "for there is neither male nor female" (Galatians 3:28b).

The golden rule, "Do unto others as you would that they will do unto you" should be the guiding principle in your treatment of your spouse. Before you know it, your children will be old enough to get married and you begin to want someone else to treat them with respect and honor. I know someone who discouraged his wife from pursuing her lifelong career because he was afraid she might be too distracted with career to settle with him. When the same thing happened to his daughter, he could not get over it. You reap what you sow.

Chapter 7

REMEMBER YOUR FIRST LOVE

When you remember the first time you met each other, it is like what Jesus described as "new wine in new wineskin" (Mark 2:22). It is a perfect state, a point where we experience love, joy and peace. When we think of the beginning of a marriage, it is imperative to consider what makes for a good relationship. What are you looking for in a spouse? Character and integrity or reputation and influence?

Character/Integrity

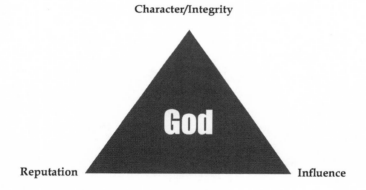

Reputation   Influence

Figure 2: Relationship

Character lies within a person. It is another term for personality. It is what an individual is made of, which may be visible or not. When we talk of traits, we refer to nature or nurture. That means that one's character is a reflection of what is inborn or acquired in the course of training and interactions with the physical and social environment.

Children have the tendency to associate with peers in a free and secure state, since they consider everyone as the same. However, when a trusted adult teaches a child that people are different due to tribe, race, social class, abilities or disabilities, that child could imbibe the negative traits of reticence, racism and nepotism. On the other hand, character could be built up when person repents and accepts Christ as Lord and Savior; he or she begins to learn by studying the Bible and praying. We must study in sincerity with a teachable heart, so that we can see others as those made in the image and likeness of God. Therefore, character evolves when it is exposed to the environment.

Integrity is virtue that shows in a character who is aware of God's presence everywhere. Integrity is synonymous with honesty, truth, truthfulness, honor, veracity, reliability and uprightness. As such, we can liken it to Christlikeness. It is morality at its highest level. One's level of integrity determines how the person behaves, whether alone or with people. In fact, it doesn't matter the caliber of people he deals with. A man of integrity is consistent in his interrelationships at all times. This is often a place of conflict in life. Character and integrity are the core of healthy marital relationships. Meanwhile, God is at the apex, overseeing and directing everything. Every marriage is strengthened by integrity.

Influence and reputation are external elements that can change at any time. When these change, the person with integrity and character remains stable. These are like 'faith, hope and love; but the greatest is love' (1 Corinthians 13:13) because love endures all things, just like integrity. The man of integrity is "he that swears to his own hurt, and changes not..." (Psalm 15:4). Can you trust your spouse?

Yes! Even when a marriage is passing through thorns and thistles, integrity stands strong. It does not give up. It is important to build integrity before and during marriage, because trials will surely come. Victories and testimonies follow character, no matter how long they last. Integrity enables one to manifest the fruit of the spirit (Galatians 5:21,22) during the most turbulent times. The man or woman of integrity will not forsake their own. You do not leave your partner in the fire (Kendrick, 2008). It takes integrity and honor to uphold your spouse in the most trying times.

Reputation and influence manifest in external or outward characteristics, such as: what part of town one lives in, where one was born, age, outward looks, how beautiful or handsome one is.

The Wiseman said, "Favor is deceitful, beauty is vain, but a woman who fears the Lord, she shall be praised" (Proverbs 31:30). It is the fear of God that establishes good character. Someone with a shady character will serve God for money; is that the kind of spouse you want? An individual with integrity will focus on truth and encourage his family to make heaven. It is a long haul. If your spouse is worldly and does not have a desire for soul-winning, he or she will likely affect your children and grieve your heart. The fear of the Lord is your safeguard.

We talk about internal and external conflicts. When these conflicts come, a person with integrity is able to say, "No" when he ought to say, "No," and "Yes," even if others are all saying, "No." He or she is true to him or herself. The worst person to deal with is the one who is so conflicted that he or she sways about to please people and is unsure what is needed. He lacks both character and integrity and cannot be relied upon. An Igbo man once said of his friend, "since he lied to help me get out of a court case, all I hear from him are lies." It's hard to know when to trust a liar.

In marriage, you want to deal with a man or woman of stable character; one that wears integrity as a garment. Then you can rely on your spouse in the most stressful times; else, your marriage vows are of no effect. A contract is only reliable when the person with whom it is made is trustworthy. Some national or state governments employ workers with the agreement to pay salaries monthly or fortnightly. Yet they owe employees for months and years. These are establishments without integrity. There is no need to make any agreement with them. Their contracts are not binding because their leaders lack both character and integrity.

For marriage to be formidable, both partners should be trusted. Nevertheless, many have married for reputation and influence. A friend recently told me of a multimillion wedding in which she participated as a friend of the family. The committee of friends wore assorted uniformed attires. It was a fiesta. They worked so hard to serve the thousands of attendees; yet the marriage itself only lasted a couple of years. Meanwhile, her own wedding which had less than twenty guests has lasted more than three decades. What a world! The wedding event does not determine the joy of marriage. Love, integrity and devotion of the couple to God will stand the test of time.

A blissful marriage is not about who the parents of your spouse are or the amount of money you are bringing into the relationship. It's not how influential any one of you is and definitely not your level of education or position in the church. Those are externals; and they fade. I remember people who married into very well-known families and, within a short time, either death or other misfortunes turned the table around. Genuine marriage may sometimes appear to be a step down from your social status. Some couples started off with nothing and today, are not only living happily but have even become more influential than those who started off as already made. Time changes everything if we are patient and persistent.

The reason for entering into a relationship is very important. It should be simple, true and unconditional love. The determination to support one another in life and ministry is easy if we stand on integrity and love. God will surely bless such a marriage. When the going gets tough, together you will stand to overcome.

Chapter 8

I VOWED

Marriage vows are based on the epistles of Paul and Peter, as well as on Jesus' message in the Gospels. Paul teaches that you are sanctified by marriage and that if your spouse is not a believer, you do not need to divorce him or her. This has more to do with two persons who got married before they came to the faith. Here you are called to win him or her over by your action. Paul did not suggest that you should go and get married outside of the faith in order to prove a point. If you were converted to Christ while married, pray for your spouse and win them to Christ.

1 Corinthians 7:10-16

> *Now to the married I command, yet not I but the Lord: A wife is not to depart from her husband. But even if she does depart, let her remain unmarried or be reconciled to her husband. And a husband is not to divorce his wife.*
>
> *But to the rest I, not the Lord, say: If any brother has a wife who does not believe, and she is willing to live with him, let him not divorce her. And a woman who has a husband who does not believe, if he is willing to live with her, let her not divorce him. For the unbelieving husband is sanctified by the wife, and the unbelieving wife is sanctified by the husband; otherwise your children would be unclean, but now they are holy. But if*

the unbeliever departs, let him depart; a brother or a sister is not under bondage in such cases. But God has called us to peace. For how do you know, O wife, whether you will save your husband? Or how do you know, O husband, whether you will save your wife?

1 Peter 3:1-7

Likewise, ye wives, be in subjection to your own husbands; that, if any obey not the word, they also may without the word be won by the conversation of the wives; while they behold your chaste conversation coupled with fear, whose adorning let it not be that outward adorning of plaiting the hair, and of wearing of gold, or of putting on of apparel; but let it be the hidden man of the heart, in that which is not corruptible, even the ornament of a meek and quiet spirit, which is in the sight of God of great price.

For after this manner in the old time the holy women also, who trusted in God, adorned themselves, being in subjection unto their own husbands: even as Sara obeyed Abraham, calling him lord: whose daughters ye are, as long as ye do well, and are not afraid with any amazement. Likewise, ye husbands, dwell with them according to knowledge, giving honour unto the wife, as unto the weaker vessel, and as being heirs together of the grace of life; that your prayers be not hindered.

You can see that humility, considering one another, respect and honor are mutual components of any relationship. No friendship works without respect and understanding. Peter particularly calls on husbands to "dwell with them according to knowledge, giving honor unto the wife as unto the weaker vessel…" (verse 7). He wants the husband to recognize the wife as also belonging "…and as being heirs together of the grace of life; that your prayers be not hindered." That means that we need one another in the race. We can benefit from recognizing the gift of God in each other. Peter views the cultural reality of his time as hindrance to prayers. It means that when you treat your wife as inferior, you are likely to miss out on many blessings. It all boils down to mutual respect and cooperation, which are acts of love.

Matthew 19:3-10

> *The Pharisees also came unto him, tempting him, and saying unto him, Is it lawful for a man to put away his wife for every cause? And he answered and said unto them, Have ye not read, that he which made them at the beginning made them male and female, and said, For this cause shall a man leave father and mother, and shall cleave to his wife: and they twain shall be one flesh?*

> *Wherefore they are no more twain, but one flesh. What therefore God hath joined together, let not man put asunder. They say unto him, Why did Moses then command to give a writing of divorcement, and to put her away? He saith unto them, Moses because of the hardness of your hearts suffered you to put away your wives: but from the beginning it was not so.*

> *And I say unto you, Whosoever shall put away his wife, except it be for fornication, and shall marry another, committeth adultery: and whoso marrieth her which is put away doth commit adultery. His disciples say unto*

him, If the case of the man be so with his wife, it is not good to marry.

In answer to the question of the Pharisees, Jesus had given this instruction. Marriage was originally meant to be permanent. Marriage sanctifies adults and keeps them safe from sexual sin; therefore, adultery and fornication are the only conditions for divorce or separation. Matthew 19:9 is a mystery that is subject to obedient interpretation: *Whosoever shall put away his wife, except it be for fornication, and shall marry another, committeth adultery: and whoso marrieth her which is put away doth commit adultery.* That's why the disciples were confused in verse 10. The carnal man cannot understand the mystery of marriage. It is too hard to fathom.

Ephesians 5:21-33

Submitting yourselves one to another in the fear of God. Wives, submit yourselves unto your own husbands, as unto the Lord. For the husband is the head of the wife, even as Christ is the head of the church: and he is the saviour of the body. Therefore as the church is subject unto Christ, so let the wives be to their own husbands in everything. Husbands, love your wives, even as Christ also loved the church, and gave himself for it; that he might sanctify and cleanse it with the washing of water by the word, that he might present it to himself a glorious church, not having spot, or wrinkle, or any such thing; but that it should be holy and without blemish.

So ought men to love their wives as their own bodies. He that loveth his wife loveth himself. For no man ever yet hated his own flesh; but nourisheth and cherisheth it, even as the Lord the church: for we are members of his body, of his flesh, and of his bones. For this cause shall a man leave his father and mother, and shall be joined unto his wife, and they two shall be one flesh. This is a great mystery: but I speak concerning Christ and the church. Nevertheless let every one of you in particular so love his wife even as himself; and the wife see that she reverence her husband.

Truly, love and submission must go together. Submission is not subjugation. Wives should submit in everything. In the vow, wives pledge to obey their husbands. This is an act of love. When love is missing from either end, submission automatically stops. Also, husbands pledge to love and honor their wives in reverence to God. When trust is missing in a relationship, the husband will no longer love and honor the wife. That goes to say that we earn respect and it is reciprocal. We have to stand by our pledge to love each other.

Genesis 2:24 says, *Therefore, a man shall leave his father and mother and be joined to his wife, and they shall become one flesh.*

Titus 2: 4,5
> *...that they admonish the young women to love their husbands, to love their children, to be discreet, chaste, homemakers, good, obedient to their own husbands, that the word of God may not be blasphemed.*

Ephesians 5:32 affirms the marriage mystery:

> *This is a great mystery, but I speak concerning Christ and the church.*

The husband is called to leave his father and mother and cling to his wife so they become one flesh. Then he is to give himself to his wife just as Christ did for the church. It is a great responsibility to present your family to God and love your wife as yourself. This is ever so difficult and I wish most young men consider this before they go on to propose to their friends. Titus' admonition reminds us to uphold the testimony of Christ by our action, so we do not give the world a chance to profane the word of God (Titus 2: 4, 5).

Carnal versus spiritual-mindedness(1 Corinthians 7 :1-16)
To avoid sexual immorality, have your own wife or husband. Your spouse was given authority over your body, so *do not deprive one another* (v.5), except for fasting and prayer. Paul advises that if you cannot exercise self-control, then you should marry (v. 9). More so, you should keep your marriage vows:

The wife is not to depart from her husband (v. 10)

Issue about divorce and remarriage (v. 11)

Let her not divorce him (v.12, 13)

Unbelieving husband is sanctified by the wife (v.14)

Saving each other (vs. 15,16)

1 Corinthians 7:3

> *Let the husband render to his wife the affection due her
> and likewise the wife to the husband.*

What does it mean to render the affection due to one
another? We should love each other in practical terms.
Affection is not just in words but also in our attitude
towards each other.

Affection is a gentle feeling of fondness or liking. It is the
act or process of affecting or being affected. One example
of affection in the Oxford online Dictionary is to be lonely
and crave affection. Affection speaks of care and
tenderness. It shows or demonstrates the emotion of love
or the state of liking for one person or the other. The
feeling of loneliness is conquered in the face of affection.
When a person is alone, receiving a call, a card, a gift, a
letter, or other act of care, the person brightens up
and feels wanted. That's why the Igbo people would say,
'how are you? can cure sickness." Sure, love is beyond the
question of 'how are you?' or the expression, 'I love you.'
Although that could still improve relationships, that's not
all it takes to live happily together. Marriage takes
absolute commitment. It means staying in and clinging to
one another at all times.

A couple got married and, after one year, had no child yet.
They were not bothered about childbearing; but a
concerned pastor called them for a discussion. In the
process, he discovered that they had never consummated
their marriage. Just as they did during courtship, they had
difficulty with breaking the boundaries of 'not holding or
touching.' Each of them was busy preserving his or her
body.

They were not sexually attracted to each other even after one year together. The pastor had the onerous task of counseling and teaching them to understand how to show affection. Their relationship was not romantic and they never imagined having it so.

It is not unholy to show erotic affection within the confines of marriage. Paul refers to it as "affection due" to each of you. 1 Corinthians 7:4 tells us that after the marriage vows are taken, "the wife does not have authority over her own body, but the husband does. And likewise the husband does not have authority over his own body, but the wife does." This could be a hard concept to grasp. But it is another aspect of mutual submission. Therefore, we are asked not to deprive one another except with consent for a short time. The conditions are: when you need to pray and fast or if someone is unwell. Paul recognizes the fact that if we are separated from each other or left in loneliness, it becomes more difficult to keep away from temptations. He calls it lack of self-control. When people are lonely or feel emotionally deprived, they desire to be affirmed. It is easy to go out looking for relationships. When spouses prefer to spend their time away from each other, they widen the gap between them, which can lead the man or woman into the arms of another, who is ready to grant him or her affection. This is what Paul warns against. Sometimes, a former relationship resurfaces or a person with an emotional problem emerges to cause them to develop support for each other. In the midst of that, the marriage will begin to crumble.

Many spouses have complained way into marriage of being emotionally incompatible. They do not enjoy mutual affection and cannot have peaceful conversations together. The truth is that most of these may have been overlooked from the time of courtship. A common cause of this is gap in age, spirituality, education and/or family background. When a godly devoted disciple of Christ gets married to a carefree, nonchalant Christian or, worse still, a nonbeliever, there will likely be arguments and disagreements on the minutest matter. Even how to show affection may be a source of disagreement. When children come, child upbringing will become a snare due to differences in values. Yes, lack of agreement on what constitutes morals will always cause tension in the home.

The worst idea is to be a hypocrite in a bid to please your intending spouse. Marriage is not an end in itself. It is the beginning of a protracted phase of life. Fondness is only one important reason to get married. It is not all that is needed. "Nevertheless because of sexual immorality, let each man have his own wife, and let each woman have her own husband." In simple term, this means *to avoid lust and sin, marry!*

The problem now comes when married people are lusting after others outside of their matrimonial relationship. Meanwhile, the marriage vow mandates that you "keep only unto him or her." Paul tells Timothy, "Flee also youthful lusts: but follow righteousness, faith, charity, peace, with them that call on the Lord out of a pure heart" (2Timothy 2:22).

Jesus equates lusts with adultery: "But I say to you that whoever looks at a woman to lust for her has already committed adultery with her in his heart" (Matthew 5:28). Isn't it worrisome that a married man will begin to regret that he did not marry a different woman he had dated or proposed to many years back? A wife could be quick to remind her husband and friends that she should have married someone else. This calls for repentance, because after the exchange of vows, your affection should be directed and limited to your spouse alone with total devotion. Each of you should strengthen the other and keep one another from lust and sin. As Paul states, "but if they cannot exercise self-control, let them marry. For it is better to marry than to burn with passion" (1 Corinthians 7:9). So, marriage is the safe haven for romance and sexual intercourse. Any practice of these outside of legal marriage is sinful and calls for repentance and renewal.

The destructive nature of the sin of adultery is why we are reminded that it is the sin within the body: "Flee sexual immorality. Every sin that a man does is outside the body, but he who commits sexual immorality sins against his own body" (1 Cor. 6:18). Though sin is sin, sexual sin has far reaching effects. We must keep the marriage bed undefiled: "Marriage is honorable among all, and the bed undefiled; but fornicators and adulterers God will judge" (Heb. 13:4).

Some desperate immigrants arrive in the United States and are ill-advised to divorce their wives and remarry someone else in order to obtain documents to remain in the country. Then when they become citizens, they divorce the transitory wife and get remarried to their real wives at home. After that, they invite their real wives over as fiancées or wives. This is simply fraud and a lot of people have committed it.

Many who compromised the sanctity of their marriages, have also lost their peace and love. During that long uncertain process of forgeries and lies, some have lost the one true relationship they had. One woman lost everything; soon after she got her immigration normalized, she got sick and did not survive. You cannot gain the whole world and lose your soul. Marriage is not a safe ground for gambling. Keep your marriage pure and holy. Trust God for sustaining your family. Do not play around for the love of money or lust for pleasure. Marriage is honorable and holy. Keep it so.

Chapter 9

PORTRAYING CHRIST IN MARRIAGE

Christ transforms our relationships. Becoming a Christian means living the new life. It means daring to be different as we pursue a life of love and holiness.

Ephesians 6: 1-9

> *Children, obey your parents in the Lord, for this is right. Honor your father and mother – which is the first commandment with a promise, "so that it may go well with you and that you may enjoy long life on the earth." Fathers, do not exasperate your children; instead, bring them up in the training and instruction of the Lord. Slaves, obey your earthly masters with respect and fear, and with sincerity of heart, just as you would obey Christ. Obey them not only to win their favor when their eye is on you, but as slaves of Christ, doing the will of God from your heart. Serve wholeheartedly, as if you were serving the Lord, not people, because you know that the Lord will reward each one for whatever good they do, whether they are slave or free. And masters, treat your slaves in the same way. Do not threaten them, since you know that he who is both their Master and yours is in heaven, and there is no favoritism with him.*

Wives submit to your **OWN** husbands as to the Lord.

1 Peter 3:1-6

> *Wives, in the same way submit yourselves to your own husbands so that, if any of them do not believe the word, they may be won over without words by the behavior of their wives, when they see the purity and reverence of your lives. Your beauty should not come from outward adornment, such as elaborate hairstyles and the wearing of gold jewelry or fine clothes. Rather, it should be that of your inner self, the unfading beauty of a gentle and quiet spirit, which is of great worth in God's sight. For this is the way the holy women of the past who put their hope in God used to adorn themselves. They submitted themselves to their own husbands, like Sarah, who obeyed Abraham and called him her lord. You are her daughters if you do what is right and do not give way to fear.*

As we review and reflect on these scriptures, we receive instructions on living together in the family. The relationship between husband and wife is the mystery of love, which calls for accountability. Each person in the home should contribute to the success of marriage. Therefore, we must note the following key points from Ephesians 5:23,24:

The husband is the head of the wife as Christ is to the Church. The Church is His body, He is the Savior of the Church; so as the Church submits to Christ, wives should submit to their husbands.

Once again, submission does not mean to allow oppression or for the husband to always have his way. The wife is not to yield to committing sin or work against her conscience. It doesn't mean to lie or conceal truth and justice or to maltreat and oppress others together. It is not to give or take bribes. The story of Ananias and his wife, Sapphira (Acts 5) shows that God is not pleased when marriage becomes a connivance for evil. Rather, the wife should submit to her husband in everything. That's why it is important who you end up with. You cannot compromise your faith on the platter of marriage.

Do not be yoked together with unbelievers. For what do righteousness and wickedness have in common? Or what fellowship can light have with darkness? What harmony is there between Christ and Belial? Or what does a believer have in common with an unbeliever? What agreement is there between the temple of God and idols? For we are the temple of the living God. As God has said: "I will live with them and walk among them, and I will be their God, and they will be my people." Therefore, "Come out from them and be separate, says the Lord. Touch no unclean thing, and I will receive you." And, "I will be a Father to you, and you will be my sons and daughters," says the Lord Almighty. 2 Corinthians 6: 14 -18

Marrying someone who does not share the same faith with you is like laying a faulty foundation that will not stand the test of time. That level of spiritual compromise will lead to regrets. So, who have you married? If you are already married, you need to win your spouse to the Lord and keep each other living for the Lord. The scriptures teach submission, no matter who your spouse is.

> *Wives, in the same way submit yourselves to your own husbands so that, if any of them do not believe the word, they may be won over without words by the behavior of their wives.* (1Peter 3:1)

Mutual submission will save your marriage. Communication will stabilize your relationship. There should be mutual respect; the golden rule should direct all your dealings.

Husbands should love their wives, as Christ loved the church (Ephesians 5: 25 -27). Jesus loves the church, so he gave himself for it, in order to sanctify and cleanse the church by the washing of water by the word. He wants to present the church to himself a glorious church without spot or wrinkle. Marriage should be holy and without blemish. That's what God wants in Christian marriage: Spotless. Peaceful. Holy. Wholesome. The husband is a type of Jesus in the marriage. And the wife is the church that must be without spot or wrinkle. Husbands should love their wives as their own bodies (vs. 28-32). If you love your wife, you love yourself; *for no one hated his own flesh, but nourishes and cherishes it, even as the Lord does His church* (Ephesians 5:29).

We are members of His body; in marriage, man and woman become one, just like Christ and his church. We know a Christian family as a unit or home consisting of a husband and wife with their children. Christian marriage is instituted to function according to biblical principles. It is a union between one man and one woman (Genesis 2:24, Matthew 19:4,5). There is no room for multiple wives or husbands. Neither is a 'marriage' between two men or two women. These negate biblical principles and could be called something else other than marriage. Christian marriage is a covenant between one man and one woman for life.

All the same, we live in a fallen world; hence, Christians also struggle in their marriages. Despite the difficulties, however, both partners in a Christian marriage are called to portray Christ in their home. They should be ready to forgive each other, and willing to be obedient to God and his word. Couples ought to be faithful to each other even when the going gets tough. The couple should strive to honor God in their relationship. God gives the grace to do so when we ask him. (Oguike, 2019). In spite of our imperfections, God provides strength for the journey as we pray daily and dwell in His presence.

> *Therefore, since we have a great high priest who has ascended into heaven, Jesus the Son of God, let us hold firmly to the faith we profess. For we do not have a high priest who is unable to empathize with our weaknesses, but we have one who has been tempted in every way, just as we are — yet he did not sin. Let us then approach God's throne of grace with confidence, so that we may receive mercy and find grace to help us in our time of need.* (Hebrews 4:14-16)

In Deuteronomy 6: 5-6, God instructs parents:

> *You shall love the Lord your God with all your heart and with all your soul and with all your might. And these words that I command you today shall be on your heart. You shall teach them diligently to your children, and shall talk of them when you sit in your house, and when you walk by the way, and when you lie down, and when you rise.*

In marriage there should be no room for selfishness. A Christian marriage exemplifies the relationship between Christ and the church (Ephesians 5:32). Christ gave himself up for the church; likewise, husbands should give themselves up for their wives and love them as their own bodies (Ephesians 5:25-29). *And as the church submits to Christ; likewise, wives should submit to their husbands and acknowledge him as the head of the family* (vs. 22-24). There is no room for selfishness. Couples are asked to honor each other (1 Peter 3:2,7). Hence, the Christian marriage replicates the bond between Christ and his church, which demonstrates mutual love, faithfulness and a servant-attitude. This love for God will guide family life and children's upbringing.

The wife should support and respect her husband like the virtuous woman of Proverbs 31:10: *A wife of noble character who can find? She is worth far more than rubies. Her husband has full confidence in her and lacks nothing of value.*

Marriage is not just about husband and wife. Children and other relatives also contribute to the progress and stability of the family. The duty of the couple is to keep everyone together in harmony. When at home, find a convenient time for daily prayers. These days, we should socialize with our family members and, where necessary, use electronic and social media, such as individual/group text/email, WhatsApp group, Snapchat, Instagram, Facebook family Group, and Twitter, when physical interaction is not possible or convenient. These media sources help us to keep up with regular individual calls when they're gone from home. Families can hold regular prayers on Skype, Zoom or other video meeting platforms. Family prayer is a necessity because it's the opportunity to keep all members together and improve family relationship. When there is harmony in the household, marriage thrives.

When there is turbulence in the home, marital bliss is hindered. Therefore, you should discuss the causes of tension in the family, starting from small matters to major ones:

Small matters

- o housekeeping

Major Issues

- o adultery, financial mismanagement, criminal offences.

- o Violence

- o Influence of outsiders

- o Influence of extended family members

- o Parents in-law – issue of control, taking either sides

- o Brother/sister-in-law

- o Grandparents - taking sides with grandkids

- o Extra people in the house – relatives, workers or friends

If problems arise and they are not resolved, there will not be lasting joy in the home. Remember that:

> *...a man leaves his father and mother and is united to his wife, and they become one flesh.* (Genesis 2:24)

For this reason a man will leave his father and mother and be united to his wife, and the two will become one flesh.' So they are no longer two, but one flesh. Therefore what God has joined together, let no one separate. (Mark 10:7)

For this reason a man will leave his father and mother and be united to his wife, and the two will become one flesh. This is a profound mystery — but I am talking about Christ and the church. However, each one of you also must love his wife as he loves himself, and the wife must respect her husband. (Ephesians 5:31)

A Christian family is a home where Jesus is honored in prayer and family members respect and honor one another. Such a home begins with a strong marriage, in which the couple truly stand on their vows. They know that our true master is the Lord Jesus Christ, to whom we are all accountable; to whom we shall give account of how we lived here on earth. Our prayer is that when he returns, he will find us faithful.

Chapter 10

LEAVING AND CLEAVING

The fundamental principle of marriage is to leave the old life and cleave to a new one. The extent of leaving and cleaving determines the success or failure of a marriage. When you get married, you forge along to begin a brand new family.

> *For this cause a man shall leave his father and mother and shall cleave to his wife and they shall become one flesh.* (Genesis 2:24).

> *But at the beginning of creation God made them male and female. For this cause a man will leave his father and mother and be united to his wife and the two will become one flesh. So they are no longer two but one. Therefore, what God has joined together, let man not separate.* (Mark 10:6-8)

There are three clear steps that must be taken when two persons get married: The man and woman must *leave*. Then they must *cleave* together. If they take these two steps, they will *become* one flesh. To leave is to depart or move away from. It also means to withdraw from or to move on (Webster, Merriam Webster Dictionary, 2020).

The call is to leave parents; however in our experience, there is much more to leave than just father and mother. Marriage is a new beginning of two individuals becoming one. Leaving parents is a difficult choice. Just like many other hard sayings of Jesus, it calls for obedience. *If anyone comes to me and does not hate his father and mother, his wife and children, his brothers and sisters — yes, even his own life — he cannot be my disciple* (Luke 14:26). Or, *Go, sell your possessions and give to the poor, and you will have treasure in heaven. Then come, follow me* (Matthew 19:21).

In Matthew 10:37, the phrase, *and hate not*, expresses the true meaning of this word, when Jesus says, *He who loveth his father and mother more than me.*

Apart from parents, other people or activities with the potential for interference in your relationship that you may need to *leave* are: friends, extended family, a sport, a hobby, activity, selfish ways, and anything else that might come in the way of our ability to bond with one another.

How should you leave?

> We must leave physically
>
> We must leave emotionally
>
> We must leave financially
>
> We must leave old loyalties or authorities
>
> We must leave our comfort zone
>
> We must leave former direction

You cannot *cleave* until you *leave*. Yet, it takes God's grace to completely leave in order to cleave.

I remember the charlatan lawyers in our city centers with billboards **advertisements** that read like this:

Want a divorce?

Call us today

It's quick and easy

Spouse's consent not needed

Figure 3: Billboard

Whenever, I read such billboards, I remember Ruth, the Moabite, who clung to her husband beyond their marriage. After her husband's death, she said to Naomi, her mother in-law:

> *Intreat me not to leave thee, or to return from following after thee: for whither thou goest, I will go; and where thou lodgest, I will lodge: thy people shall be my people, and thy God my God.* (Ruth 1: 16)

At most evangelical church weddings in the 1980s, the bridal marching song was:

> *I will not leave my Lord*
>
> *Where he goeth, I will go*
>
> *Where he liveth, I will live*
>
> *His people shall be mine*
>
> *I will not leave my Lord*
>
> *Where he goeth, I will go*
>
> *O my Lord, guide my way and see me through*

For a successful marriage, you need to cling to the Lord, cleave to the solid foundation, obey God's command and submit to one another. The Lord is our anchor for a successful marriage. Every day, you must return to the Lord in prayers, seeking him and worshipping him together with clean hearts.

You should reflect on your Christian calling: Are you heaven-bound or is your hope only on this earth? Your response will determine where your marriage is headed. Remember, *if only in this life we have hope in Christ, we are to be pitied more than all men* (1Corinthians 15:19). Therefore, we are part of the body of Christ and his bride.

Cleaving

To cleave is to adhere firmly and closely or loyally and unwaveringly (Webster, Merriam Webster Dictionary, 2020). Cleaving means to remain faithful, to cleave to one's principle in spite of persecution. It is a demonstration of faith, trust and belief. Thus, leaving and cleaving form the foundation of a successful marriage. Without these, families will be at risk of tension.

The challenges of cleaving

The wise woman builds her house, but with her own hands the foolish one tears hers down (Proverbs 14:1).

So, does a wise man. Your marriage or home is an edifice you are building. Of what substance is your house being built? I have seen women face serious obstacles in their marriages and still stand, because of the wisdom from God. Are you too busy to cleave? We ought to build together with the same vision and mission.

> *According to the grace of God which is given unto me, as a wise master builder, I have laid the foundation, and another buildeth thereon. But let every man take heed how he buildeth thereupon. For other foundation can no*

man lay than that is laid, which is Jesus Christ. Now if any man build upon this foundation gold, silver, precious stones, wood, hay, stubble; Every man's work shall be made manifest: for the day shall declare it, because it shall be revealed by fire; and the fire shall try every man's work of what sort it is. (1 Cor. 3: 10 – 13).

Be a responsible builder. Build your home or house. Build your bank account and strengthen your children together. Endeavor to discover your individual and joint callings and support each other. Aim to reveal the best of yourselves.

In order for a couple to truly bond, there must be *agape,* God's kind of love. This kind of love encompasses spiritual, emotional and physical balance. We achieve this by talking sincerely, walking together, and dating regularly. Just as intimacy with God is developed through prayers and the study of his word, intimacy with one's spouse is developed and strengthened by deliberately spending time together to understand each other.

Communication

Couples should share their lives together by sincerely expressing their inner feelings. They should not keep anger till dusk, nor sweep garbage under the carpet. Rather, they should share their concerns with one another. Each one will live in denial and refuse to be selfish and self-centered.

Spouses ought to be sincere about personal health situations, finances, friends and family. At the end of each day, do a heart to heart sharing of your day and activities as you work together through life. Nevertheless, you should respect each other's individuality. It is important to always remember that you are from different backgrounds. That means you may:

have different gifts and talents

have different professions

have gender-related feelings

have your own opinions

have your moods change for different reasons

not understand his or her jokes

not feel free with his or her 'weird' friends and relatives

Hence, you should be understanding of your differences and try to learn how to keep bonding. It calls for leveraging your strengths and helping each other to overcome weaknesses.

Let me reemphasize the practice of praying together, which is the only way we receive strength for the walk ahead. You truly cannot pray together and still bear grudges against each other or complain about yourselves to other people.

> *Two are better than one, because they have a good return for their work: If one falls down, his friend can help him up. But pity the man who falls and has no one to help him up!* (Ecclesiastes 4:9,10)

Let's remain faithful to the Lord before whom you made a solemn vow. Be a faithful and trustworthy spouse. That's why we ask unmarried and engaged couples to make sure they are in love enough to go the extra mile. Surely, your convictions shall be tried and tested. The ability to hold onto each other and remain faithful till death is called cleaving. Are you cleaving?

Chapter 11

IN SICKNESS AND IN HEALTH

When we make our vows at the altar before God
 and the congregation of His people, most of us
are not thinking of sickness and disease. In fact,
the generality of brides and grooms are rather fantasizing
about blissful life that will continue to a ripe old age. No
wonder most modern day vows will include, "you are the
one I want to grow old with." As sweet as that sounds,
many marriages do not get to that good old age. A major
percentage of those that remain together till older age are
no longer as delightful as was expected.

One reason marriage relationships wane is that the
human body begins to go through changes as years go by,
due to the aging process. More often than not, sickness
creeps in and alter everything. A few people come into
marriage already sick. When that is the case, it is
necessary to be plain with your friend even before
accepting to go into courtship.

In communities where sickle cell anemia is a problem,
two individuals who have the sickle cell trait are seriously
advised not to get married. As such, it is better to share
such health issue with your spouse before betrothal so
that you can take the best decision for your future.

The question would then be: "should we marry or not?"
With all the facts before you, take a decision fully aware of

the challenges. Most couples get to middle-age before the monster of ill health begins to rear up its head. When your spouse starts slowing down and losing interest in some of the things you both did together, you feel bad and are demoralized by the unwanted changes. Of course, you are bound to react. How you respond to the change is a demonstration of your depth of love and empathy for your loved one. It also reflects your dedication to God.

In Christian marriage, prayer is key to staying together. It constantly reminds you of your vows which you made before you got married. Through prayers and walking together, you will learn to adapt to all the lifestyle changes.

Without spiritual and emotional maturity, some spouses begin to hide their problems. If you are sick and will not share it with your husband or wife, you are likely to be without the right support system that you will need when the time comes. It shows a lack of trust and a feeling of insecurity on your part. No one causes his or her own sickness; no one should, therefore, feel guilty for being sick. Rather, we should be genuine and open. In that case, no one should be thinking you are pretending to be tired and cannot help as you used to. If doctors and nurses will know what is wrong with you, why would you hide it from your family? When you are open, both of you can work things out together.

I know of parents who have hidden underlying ill-health from their children and are watching them make the same mistakes that led their parents to the point where they are. However, the vows we made are to be together in sickness and in health. You should not abandon your spouse because of sickness. That is the time to be by him or her and pray until they bounce back to good health or God take them home. That's what you vowed to do. It is immoral to abandon your partner when he or she needs you most.

Bode and Iris were best friends who got married in a romantic adventure of their time. After a classy society wedding, they moved across the continent to enjoy their happily ever-after life. We all thought it was a fairy tale marriage. The next time I heard of them was two decades after. By then, Bode was dead. I could not believe it. He had died in his prime because Iris had expected life to be a bed of roses and could not bear it otherwise. I do not have all the details of this matter, but I learned that each time there was stress in their home, Iris left Bode to stay alone. During one of their separations, he got very sick. She would leave him alone and travel to celebrate her milestones with her friends and their families. Bode felt lonely in the midst of sickness while in a foreign land. All these led to permanent separation. He became very sick and was living alone. One day, Iris got a call that Bode had collapsed in his apartment and had been rushed to the hospital. Before she could get there, he was already in a coma and did not recover from it.

The truth is that, when I spoke to Iris, she could not clearly articulate what happened to her husband. She was seriously stricken and now wishes she could turn back the hand of the clock and have her husband back. Alas, it is too late!

Meanwhile, Nse's husband has been sick for twenty years now. Despite her very distinguished career, she makes him priority number one. Inyang has had various medical procedures at home and abroad. At a point, he had to stop work and eventually retire; but Nse has always been by his side. He was going to be sent to a nursing home to have "professionals" take care of him, but Nse would have none of that. She kept hearing, "for better, for worse, in sickness and in health" as she considered every suggestion on how to take care of her ailing husband. She had long pledged to be the support that Inyang would need and did it so diligently that it marveled everyone. She is the example of the virtuous woman, whose husband is honored in the city gate (Proverbs 31:23). Even in sickness, Inyang was kept clean and well-groomed. He put on a smile and lived because he knew that he was much loved.

Love bears all things, believes all things, hopes all things, endures all things. Love never fails (1Corinthians 13:7, 8a).

As a couple today, Inyang and Nse have seen all their children get married and some of them have children. They continue to celebrate 'until death parts them'. When someone feels abandoned, there is nothing to live for. Yet, sickness does not mean death. It doesn't show that a person is no longer useful to the family. The tribal storyteller of your family may be a person on a wheel chair and continues to pass down the history and tradition of the community to the next generation. He or she is an asset to the family and the society at large. So, sickness or disability should never be a reason to abandon your spouse. Give each other what you need to keep functioning.

If your spouse can no longer function as before, begin to build his new strengths. Look for his abilities and not his weaknesses and harness his ingenuity. Provide him all the needed support. Most people are actually incapacitated for a short time; hence, with prayers and encouragement, they get out of their condition. Do not join the devil to kill your spouse. Give life by standing by him or her, for better for worse!

Chapter 12

DO UNTO OTHERS

Now these things were our examples, to the intent
we should not lust after evil things, as they also
lusted. Neither be ye idolaters, as were some of
  them; as it is written, The people sat down to eat and
  drink, and rose up to play. Neither let us commit
  fornication, as some of them committed, and fell in one
  day three and twenty thousand.

Neither let us tempt Christ, as some of them also tempted,
and were destroyed of serpents. Neither murmur ye, as
some of them also murmured, and were destroyed of the
destroyer. Now all these things happened unto them for
examples: and they are written for our admonition, upon
whom the ends of the world are come. Wherefore let him
that thinketh he standeth take heed lest he fall. (1
Corinthians 10:6 -12)*

A few women are as deeply spiritual as Kayla. She had
lived honestly and honorably with her husband until all
their children grew up and left home. They were two busy
professionals who hardly found enough time for the
simple pleasures of life. One day, Kayla received a phone
call from Allen, her long forgotten bosom friend from her
youth. She was so excited to meet and reconnect with
him; they talked and laughed about the past. Within one
week, they were talking and exchanging messages almost

every day. Although they did not see each other, their former relationship was totally rekindled. Kayla remembered that Allen had wanted to marry her and began to sense an intense reawakening of passion. She was scared that it could lead to sin. Not only was she a child of God, she was happily married and responsible for the life and spiritual growth of many believers.

These days of social media, messages, photos, videos and emoji flooded her phone from her erstwhile friend. She learned that he had not been prosperous in marriage. Allen blamed all his misfortunes on not marrying Kayla back in their youthful days.

From a spiritual perspective, Kayla was ready to talk with him, advise him and pray for him; but soon she realized that Allen would not leave her alone. He wanted to talk to her, to see her and to reconnect with her at all costs. He went ahead to confess that he will not be able to control himself if he sees her again. At that point, Kayla felt violated. She knew she could be playing with fire and had to stop immediately. Meanwhile, Allen seemed stuck in the past, and that frightened Kayla. She kept struggling with the fear that Allen was unhappy and could get hurt if she shunned him. She tried to get him to understand that there must be boundaries in marriage; but he was not interested in restrictions. Instead, he gave her examples of other minister-friends who still associated closely with their past friends of the opposite gender, even though they were men and women of God. After she talked with an elderly Christian sister, Kayla had no choice than to block Allen's phone numbers. She did that and restored her sanity.

When you relate to people outside of your marriage, you have to consider the purity of your thoughts;

> *Finally, brethren, whatsoever things are true, whatsoever things are honest, whatsoever things are just, whatsoever things are pure, whatsoever things are lovely, whatsoever things are of good report; if there be any virtue, and if there be any praise, think on these things.* (Philippians 4:8).

When a married woman gets preoccupied with calling another woman's husband and keeping him on the phone for hours and vice versa, they are either emotionally attached or could get so connected that they begin to compare the other with their spouses. Impure thoughts will show up and may result in sinful acts. The scriptures will judge the intents of the heart. Jesus warns, "But I say to you that whoever looks at a woman to lust for her has already committed adultery with her in his heart" (Matthew 5:28).

The Holy Spirit will lead us into all truth, so we can seek God's face and direction in all our relationships. In Kayla's case, she kept praying about her actions. She prayed so fervently and sincerely that the Lord began to guide her step by step. She prayed for Allen and his wife, knowing that something must be amiss with their relationship, because he seemed to prefer others' company to that of his wife. Kayla could not keep that friendship because her conscience would not allow her to offend another woman. She imagined that she would not like her husband to be crushing on another man's wife as Allen has been on her.

While Kayla was praying and considering her actions, hoping she was not being prideful and judgmental, she saw a vision of Allen, which frightened her. He looked so disgusting when he appeared to her and seemed to be stalking her in a creepy manner. Kayla was sick to her stomach. She hadn't seen him for ages; and now he appeared to her looking like a monster. That was it! That proved to her that any friendship with him would be of no good. She was convinced that she took the right decision not to have any more conversations with him. She reached out to her prayer partner and they prayed on the matter. She kept him out of her life without any thought against him. Allen would not take a "No" for an answer; he continued to try to get her attention. But Kayla reminded him that she belonged to her husband through the covenant of marriage and will not give heed to any negative emotion. More so, she knew that "…whatever you want men to do to you, do also to them, for this is the Law and the Prophets" (Matthew 7:12). Kayla returned to her husband and talked it over with him and they prayed together.

Who are the others in your marriage? Your fellow men or colleagues? Your fellow women, the wife of another man or husband of the other woman you met? The tempter, seducer or seductress? You do not want a sinner to die in his or her sin; respect their boundaries. Do not covet another man's wife or husband. Keep yourself pure.

When Javier's wife was pregnant, he found himself flirting after one of his church ladies, Adua. She was uncomfortable each time Javier came visiting her and often rebuked him. But in self-pity, he tried to explain that he was lonely because his wife was no longer interested in him. This annoyed Adua and she was quick to redirect him. "This is the time she actually craves your support, no matter how she shows it," she scolded. "Just go home and be patient with her." She was aggravated with him but kept praying for the couple until they had their baby and things returned to normal for them. Javier was a doubleminded believer who was carnal and hypocritical.

Despite their spirituality, these church members faced temptations. They were only able to conquer because there were praying persons among them. If all were carnally-minded, their stories would have ended in regrets, as is the case with many of the newsflashes around today. From time to time, we hear of a well-known believer or pastor who has fallen into adultery and sometimes died in the act. We hear of those indulging in pornography and other amorous acts.

Prayerlessness is a disturbing issue. Each of us must be conscious of God's presence wherever we may be in our Christian walk. "Therefore, let him who thinks he stands take heed lest he fall" (1 Corinthians 10:12). This also calls for resoluteness.

> But Daniel purposed in his heart that he would not defile himself with the portion of the king's delicacies, nor with the wine which he drank; therefore, he requested of the chief of the eunuchs that he might not defile himself. (Daniel 1:8)

The story was told of a youth who was invited to commit an immoral act with others. He was quick to respond,

"Okay, I will do it. But please, take me to a place where God will not see us, then I can do it." That was the end of the matter. No one bothered him again. Our God is omnipresent. "God is our refuge and strength, a very present help in trouble" (Psalm 46:1). So, just like the hidden camera, he is watching us and knows what is happening in our lives. Therefore, you must revere him in your heart and keep your matrimonial bed pure. Remember, "Marriage is honorable among all, and the bed undefiled; but fornicators and adulterers God will judge" (Hebrews 13:4).

Therefore, you must love and cherish the "bone of your bone" (Genesis 2:23).

Chapter 13

WHEN YOUR SPOUSE IS AWAY

In my book, *Called Together*, Chapter 8: As Light in the Society, I discussed the topic, "Staying Apart" (Martin-Oguike, 2018). While writing that in the first edition of the book published in 1998, I never imagined that I was going to soon experience being away, firsthand. In 1999, my husband proceeded on a one-year sabbatical leave from his college. That was the beginning of being away for four and a half years. Within that time, he was home three times before we finally joined him to immigrate to the United States. What does it mean to be staying apart in real life? It is a temporary, geographical separation that is often agreed upon by both spouses, for the purpose of educational, economic or ministry progression; it comes with its own level of responsibility and pressure.

In a nutshell, living separate from your spouse could be extremely stressful. It is a trying experience that reveals to each of you what kind of Christian you are. Once again, the lessons of integrity and character are relevant here, because if you have no integrity and have not built character, you are bound to fall in the day of adversity. However, "the fear of the LORD is the beginning of wisdom, and the knowledge of the Holy One is understanding" (Proverbs 9:10). That's why the Sage declares: "The wise woman builds her house, but the foolish pulls it down with her hands" (Proverbs 14:1). The choice is yours. Remembering that you are heaven-bound, you will be occupied for him/her and continue to uphold your family values until you are reunited to each other.

Despite the utter loneliness I faced at that time, I relearned self-control and rose to overcome temptations while holding up. My activities during those years deserves a book of its own. My life then was very rewarding. I realized my real personality as a wife, mother and professional. I know it's God who kept me going because there was just no way I could have achieved so much within such a short time while taking care of three children. I began and completed an MFA program at the University of Nigeria, held a joint Art Exhibition with the Society of Nigerian Artists, and a solo Art Exhibition in Umuahia. I spoke at several events in and out of the state and was involved in church planting and growing. I was actively involved with the Rural Development Organization in Umuahia Anglican Diocese; we went into villages for projects, teaching skills to women and girls. I spoke at schools and colleges' fellowship groups and was expositor at a number of Scripture Union programs, including student camp meetings. My children clung to my pouch, the Mama kangaroo! We went everywhere together.

I think I was busy and prayerful, warding off so much stress and temptation by the grace of God and the sword of the spirit, which is the word of God. I just want to say that my life was preserved in those days by the fear of God, integrity of character, business activities, love of my husband and children, which was constant and unconditional, and the support of family and the brethren. God's grace abounds for us as we remain unscathed. Yes, we looked up in hope and hope conquered. "I will lift up mine eyes unto the hills, from whence cometh my help. My help cometh from the LORD, which made heaven and earth" (Psalms 121:1-2). To live apart from each other is not bread and butter. Even the remembrance of those days is stressful till date.

Odia's wife traveled abroad to complete a degree program, while he took care of their children. He was so magnanimous and did a great job of giving those children the best foundation in life. When Neki graduated and returned from abroad, the youngest who was an infant when she left, was already four. Life soon returned to the old happy way. Several years after, as they continued to grow in their profession, she decided to apply for a grant to pursue a doctoral program abroad. Odia would hardly refuse Neki's requests. She asked for him to purchase the forms for her and he did. They filled out the forms, posted them and waited. After many months, the response came back. Neki was given a grant to cover her studies and dissertation in Europe. Odia's eyes opened. He remembered the hardship and loneliness of those years that Neki was away. He was angry and ready to fight. Odia was not ready to go through the trauma a second time.

Yet, he did not come outrightly to oppose his wife's travel plans. He became angry and demonstrated it in their daily activities. I gathered from both of them that all was not well. Neki knew he did not want her to leave again, but then it was he who bought the forms and paid for the tests. Odia saw me on my way to church one day and started complaining. "You'd better advise your friend, because she wants to leave us and travel again," he whined. "If she does it this time..." he threatened. I quickly challenged him, "Why did you purchase the forms and pay for the process if you didn't want her to go?" I asked.

He was taken aback. It was obvious that he was trying to let peace reign and falsely believing that she was not going to get the scholarship; but he was wrong. "Let me just tell you, Odia," I put on my teacher voice, "Go home, talk to your wife like the head of the household that you are. Tell her in clear language that you do not want her to go. My friend is a Christian and she will listen."

"You think so?" he asked doubtingly.

"Yes. If she wouldn't, then this conversation will continue." I was emphatic.

A couple of days later, it was Neki who told me that her husband no longer wanted her to travel and that she has shelved the plan. She is a woman of honor. Fortunately, God still honored her with the same degree in a different university within the country.

Separation is stressful. So speak out if you know you cannot manage it. No one deserves to die in silence. Meanwhile, it is unfair to assume that your husband or wife will not accept a point of view that you have not expressed. You have to communicate your point and have a conversation, especially in decisions that affect your entire family. Never leave each other when you have not deliberated together and worked out your plan ahead of time.

Think about other reasons that couples sometimes have to stay apart. Have you ever had to stay apart with your spouse? How were you able to remain stable during those times? Consider another couple that may be going through any type of separation at this time. Pray for them and help where you can.

Chapter 14

THAT OTHER PERSON

Hassan will always bemoan his youth as he spoke passionately about the other ladies he had desired to marry and, for some reasons, did not marry. Whenever he socialized with his peers, he would raise that topic for discussion. Even as an elderly married man, apparently happily to a woman who outshone all the other people he referred to, he would recall his escapades with his would-have-been wives—sometimes, right before his wife.

Consider the command, "...hold only unto you till death us do part." Holding unto him or her has much to do with where our emotions are. Also, it means not giving room to the enemy to attack our relationship and enjoying where we are.

On a certain occasion, I had a discussion with a gentleman who believes he made a grievous mistake in his marriage choice and now understands that he has to make the best of what he has. As the Jersey man will say, "Stay where you're at." Are you staying where you are? Is your spirit, soul and body within your marriage? It sounds easy; but often, the straying mind is the beginning of the fall of a relationship. "A doubleminded person is unstable in all his ways" (James 1:8). That's why it is important to marry someone you are sincerely in love with; someone who you respect and care about; someone you are sure loves you also.

In three decades as a pastor's wife and a mother, I know that very many couples are not so blessed to find the ideal spouse. However, many have made the decision to be the ideal spouse and so their marriages continue to thrive.

When you go on the altar and take the vow, "...for better for worse...", you are saying that you can improve this relationship and make it a place of abode, no matter what tomorrow brings. Even if you believe that you are no longer loved, you cannot just jump out of your marriage. Marriage is too sacred for one to slide in and out at will. Are you ready to follow God's word? One of my church ladies was fuming when a divorced lady was called upon to address the church women's group. She said, "No, No, No! If she wants to talk to us, let her go and reconcile with her husband. Does she think our marriages are so much fun that we are staying in?" You do not jump in and out of marriage. Look inwards and not outwards.

Marriage is a hallowed institution; the mystery of Christ and his church. It is a foretaste of the marriage supper of the lamb. This is seen in true Christian families whose members look forward to being together and feeling safe and secure with each other. When you start looking away from your spouse, everything becomes checkered. If you ever begin to compare your spouse to others, you will likely become belligerent and destroy your relationship. Such attitudes breed regrets, leading to "I shouldn't have married this person." It eventually leads to failure. It's your choice.

If ever those little foxes of regrets come into your marriage, the best thing is to turn them away by prayer and confession of sins; then begin to make extra efforts to be closer to your spouse. Things happen when you are physically or emotionally distracted from one another or when your heart is beginning to backslide from the Lord. It is much worse when you are not praying together as a couple. When such things happen, it is time to retrace your steps to your "first love." You have to recall the old wine and renew your love covenant that culminated in marriage and a pledge to live together until death separate you.

Mike had been married twice, had no children from both experiences, but swears that he had not been in love with either of his wives. He thinks he should have married someone else, who he had failed to propose to, and for which he blames himself. He believes he has to pay with a life of regret and does not know what else to do.

The main problem of many relationships is that people are obviously stuck in their past. To outgrow the past is sometimes as difficult as "repent and forsake your sins." It is easier said than done!

When I started to talk to Mike, he felt he was under a spiritual attack and I couldn't grasp the concept. I asked him to find practical ways to handle his problems, including repentance and prayers. "My brother, you need to put the past behind you, so you can move on with the future." Relationships are mostly impacted by past experiences. We need to put aside the past. That is a decision as real as becoming born again.

It is hard when you are stuck to past revelations, relationships, hurts and childhood experiences. And worse because you will be unable to ascend to the future that God has in stock for you. When you dream of the past, you cannot envision the future. It's time to move on and appreciate what you have. Put the past in its place. Think of a timeline that moves forward. If you have had a broken engagement, a divorce, been widowed, or was rejected by family and friends, and survived, you do yourself no favor by moaning over them. Rather, look ahead; press on towards the prize (Philippians 3:14). Rise up and walk!

I advised Mike to make the best of his present relationship. "Spend time with your wife so you can grow your love." As per childbearing, face the reality of life. You have to consider three options: (1) spend more time together and improve your physical, emotional and spiritual health. If God wills, He will give you your own biological children. (2) Visit your gynecologist, as there are modern fertility treatments that work. (3) Adopt a child or children that need a Christian home. God can still send your own biological children in his time. But be real.

I told him categorically that I do not like the pretentious life of self-pity. He has to find peace in sustaining a stable relationship. He needs to forgive himself for his past mistakes and be sincere with his present wife henceforth.

I reminded him that he had promised to love and cherish his wife unconditionally. Yes, you cannot have your heart elsewhere and still love your spouse unconditionally. Also, you cannot keep breaking your marriage vows until you think you've found true love. You have to enter into marriage advisedly and be completely yielded to one another. Double-mindedness is a snare and cannot sustain you. In holy wedlock, faith merges with love.

You must believe that your relationship will work because it is a covenant, not a random relationship or a probability; marriage is meant to stand. You are bound "till death," so you cannot afford not to build it on the foundation of love. If you discover that you have a shaky foundation, then find time to talk to each other. Prayerfully rebuild and fortify your foundation. Go out again; spend time with God and each other. Start afresh.

I like the idea of a "fresh start" program for the clergy. It takes place after many years of being in the ministry. I think a fresh start is also important in matrimony. Your anniversary period should be a great time for a fresh start retreat. It's time to talk; a time to reconsider your walk together and hold hands again. This should happen whenever you need it. Don't wait till you get to court before you discuss your differences. Plan a fresh start for your marriage when you need it. It's time to open up and be exposed before each other. Discuss what is working and what is not working in your relationship. Stand bare before each other without being ashamed.

Chapter 15

FRESH START

Now the Lord had said unto Abram, Get thee out
of thy country, and from thy kindred, and from
thy father's house, unto a land that I will shew
thee: and I will make of thee a great nation, and I will
bless thee, and make thy name great; and thou shalt be a
blessing: and I will bless them that bless thee, and curse
him that curseth thee: and in thee shall all families of the
earth be blessed. So Abram departed, as the Lord had
spoken unto him; and Lot went with him: and Abram was
seventy and five years old when he departed out of Haran.
And Abram took Sarai his wife, and Lot his brother's son,
and all their substance that they had gathered, and the
souls that they had gotten in Haran; and they went forth
to go into the land of Canaan; and into the land of Canaan
they came. (Gen. 12: 1 -5)

For you to bloom, you have to reflect on the positive
aspects of your relationship. You should constantly
remember your first love and keep your wine fresh like
the miracle wine at the marriage at Cana in Galilee where
the best wine remained till the end (John 2:1 -11).
Moreover, you should walk in obedience to God and
together constantly:

Do something new and exciting

Communicate deeply

Learn your love language

Spend quality time together

Establish rituals for each day

The number 2020 was like the restarting code for our lives. When we ushered in the year at the January prayer retreat, I announced that this is **the year of the family**. It sounded so routine. In my mind, I was thinking of programs for the year that will be geared towards family life, couples, marriage and so forth. We were all looking forward to an exciting year of activities as usual. In our New York ministry, we agreed to have a family life retreat and started looking for an event venue. Then the pandemic struck! Yes, the Lord had a plan to get the attention of Christian families, including mine. We were in for the wonder of the century and did not know it.

When the lockdown was announced in New York and New Jersey, we never thought it was possible, nor did we imagine it would last for more than a month. But by the second month at home, we were dumbfounded as we watched corpses of New Yorkers daily being carted away in thousands. People clung together at home and in the community. We came to the reality that life is just a breath. Fear froze the land and we all peeped out from the electronic holes in our homes, while clinging on faith in the hope that God will see us through.

The lessons of the pandemic are enduring. They are crowned by the realization that no one sticks closer than the family. My nuclear family held together as never before. We sat together, ate together, prayed together, and studied together, searching the scriptures and the internet to know what is next. Each one stood tall lending shoulder for the other to lean on. When fear approached, one person was sure to rebuke it and we trudged along. Terrible news floated across our coast and we refused to open the hedge to let it in. Obviously, God was teaching us how to be the support system for one another. After all said and done, we are here celebrating his sufficiency. More so, we celebrated the renewal of our relationship as siblings, parents, children, grand-children, grandparents, and spouses. Those months of lockdown have taught us that we really love each other. Yes, not every family could endure together, but we enjoyed one another. Truly, we did not need anyone to tell us; we learned to be one another's keeper during the year of the family.

The gates finally opened. Big lessons were learned from experiences and not from seminars. We had a fresh start that was not planned nor stage-managed. That's where we are, a new beginning and a new normal. I know we need that revitalization as often as possible.

Just as in real life functions, a fresh start is of essence in marriage. Time and again, spouses take each other for granted and continue to stretch the band until it elapses. It's like an engine that is never serviced. In order to renew your marriage and to spice it up, both of you have to agree to make it sweeter.

A fresh start program at work is often not mandatory. It is essential to the growth and stability of your career. That's why you take a leave, attend a refresher course and participate in end of year retreats.

Fresh start is a reminder of your first love, the reason you got together in the first place. It is like changing the oil of your car engine during servicing, so it begins again to operate in full gear. It's time for renewal of covenants and vows. A time to reinvent yourselves and forge onto greater heights. Just like defragmenting your computer so that all files are cleaned up, so you speed it up once again. Fresh start is a time to face new realities in your married life. As your children grow, leave for college, get married and leave home, you face the reality of less people at home. It calls for a fresh start, a retreat and a renewal.

How do you have a fresh start?

There is a time to renew your youthfulness by strengthening your prayer life together and dwelling on scriptures to support your marriage. The Bible is so complete. You could study Songs of Solomon, Ephesians, 1st Peter and other passages on love and marriage. It is time to play games, include team building activities; restore what you have in common; confess your faults, make yourself vulnerable and be ready to lend a helping hand.

Fresh start is a time to talk, touch and teach each other. It is a date like no other. Like Adam and Eve, *they were naked and not ashamed* (Genesis 2:25). It is not a time to play Mr. and Mrs. Perfect; rather, a time to hold hands, lie together, encourage each other, look back and plan forward. No matter what has transpired before now, you must find time *to have and to hold* your spouse. Yes, that's the purpose of a fresh start.

When a couple is separated due to business or/studies, a fight/quarrel, sickness/hospitalization or a total divorce and then come back together; there's need for a fresh start.

You may think of other reasons for separation and add to the list. The fresh start affords you the opportunity to discuss how the issues began and how the problem can be solved to avoid reoccurrence. You then resolve matters and get back together stronger than before. You must invest on consolidating your marriage and building a formidable family. It begins with setting yourselves apart for renewal. Many take time to think together about their marriages during landmark anniversaries. Some focus on traveling, taking photos, showing off on social media and so on. That's not what the fresh start is all about. It's looking inwards and not trying to attract attention of anyone else. It's about you and your spouse. Focus on the most essential things. Not even your parents, siblings and children can help you make your relationship better, if you decide otherwise. Press the refresh button of your marriage.

It is a time to concentrate on your relationship. You must not be too busy or too important to have time with your spouse. Many of our forebears lived in anger and loneliness over the years because they never found time to freshen their marriages after losing their first love. There must be a time to STOP! And then RESTART! It could be as regular as every day, or when you pray together daily or weekly; when you have a prayer and fasting retreat, weekly date night, during your wedding anniversary or even once in five years or more; a fresh start ensues. If you do not stop to review and improve your marriage, it will turn into what a mischievous American calls 'life sentence!' It will become an annoying dilapidated house, to say the least.

Marriage is not a 'sentence' because you willingly and lovingly embarked on it. It is a blissful trip meant to complete you and prepare you for the marriage supper of the lamb. Marriage is honorable; it is instituted by God. The marriage bed should not be defiled: *Marriage is honorable in all, and the bed undefiled: but fornicators and adulterers God will judge* (Hebrews 13:4). But the God of grace is able to restore even the most troubled marriage, if we genuinely walk with Him.

Many sincere men and women of God have gone to the extent of getting divorced. Yet, after subjecting themselves to the Holy Spirit's tutelage, they returned to their spouses, asked for forgiveness and were reconciled and remarried. This is the real fresh start with the same spouse. Just as Jesus is the spouse of the Church and continues to purify her, so we should continue to purify one another. Peter responded to the Lord with a question, "to whom shall we go, for you have the word of eternal life?" (John 6:68). Married couples who have made the vow are like the man described in Psalm 15:4, "if he has sworn to his own hurt, changeth it not." They stand on their word and, as such, put in all it takes to make the home a place of joy and laughter, no matter the circumstances around them.

Before you leap, you have to look. Take time to rethink any decision to leave your husband or wife. In the movie,

Fire Proof, by Kirk Cameron, we saw that you never leave your partner behind in the fire. The firemen returned to pull their co-firefighters from the raging fire before the explosion blew up the house. So, when your spouse is under the attack of the enemy, you cannot leave him or her. You have to go in to rescue your spouse from a life of regret before the bridegroom of the church returns.

In the most difficult time of differences, some have divorced their wedded spouses and remarried. As a Christian, what do you really need: a reconciliation or separation? Before you finalize a divorce or plan a remarriage to another spouse, it is advisable to study the following scriptures and ask the Holy Spirit to speak specifically to you:

> *It has been said, 'Anyone who divorces his wife must give her a certificate of divorce.' But I tell you that anyone who divorces his wife, except for sexual immorality, makes her the victim of adultery, and anyone who marries a divorced woman commits adultery.* (Matthew 5:31-32)

> *A woman is bound to her husband as long as he lives. But if her husband dies, she is free to marry anyone she wishes, but he must belong to the Lord. In my judgment, she is happier if she stays as she is — and I think that I too have the Spirit of God.* (1Corinthians 7:39,40)

I may not have all the revelations on this topic at this time, but from what the scriptures say, I advise you to keep your marriage hallowed and fight to keep your spouse. Except where your life is clearly in danger, do not separate or divorce your husband or wife. Marriage is sacred and divorce is an ill wind that blows no one any good — neither the couple nor the children.

Divorce could be illustrated with two bottles glued together with super glue. When they are permanently stuck, you cannot detach them without breaking one or both bottles. After you have been married and shared part or all of your life with someone else, you should be wise not to allow your relationship to end due to a flimsy decision. Think of the consequences of a broken marriage. The guilt of failure, the emotional stability of your children, the families involved and your walk with God.

At the end of a Christian wedding, the minister declares, "What God has joined together, let no one put asunder." NO ONE includes even you, the couple. If God joins together, God will put asunder at his own time. Till then, our job is to help strengthen and enable each other to enjoy the future as much as we can. That's what you pledged at the solemnization of your marriage. Therefore, go for a fresh start! Return to each other, to have and to hold.

Chapter 16

FOLLOW THE WAY

Do not let your hearts be troubled. You believe in
God; believe in Me as well. In My Father's house
are many rooms. If it were not so, would I have
told you that I am going there to prepare a place for you?
And if I go and prepare a place for you, I will come back
and welcome you into My presence, so that you also may
be where I am. You know the way to the place where I am
the Way, the Truth, and the Life. "Lord," said Thomas,
"we do not know where You are going, so how can we
know the way?" Jesus answered, "I am the way and the
truth and the life. No one comes to the Father except
through Me. If you had known Me, you would know My
Father as well. From now on you do know Him and have
seen Him." (John 14: 1-7)

Jesus has gone to prepare us a place and will return to
receive and take us to the place, so we will be with Him.
Thomas then questioned Jesus in verse 5, "Lord, we do
not know where you are going, and how can we know the
way." I like Thomas. He always needed clarification and
was not ashamed to ask for it. He always asked the
clarifying question, which led to Jesus' profound
declaration in verse 6, "I am the Way, the Truth, and the
Life. No one comes to the Father except through Me."
That is in line with Acts 4:12, where Peter said, "Nor is

there salvation in any other, for there is no other name under heaven given among men by which we must be saved." Also, 1 Timothy 2:5 states, "For there is one God, and one mediator between God and men, the Man Christ Jesus."

Jesus continued to explain to Philip and other disciples that anyone that has seen him has seen God the Father. And the Father dwells in him and works through him (verses 9 and 10).

The results of believing in Jesus are:

1. "The works I do he will do also, and greater works than these he will do" (verse 12). Generations of men and women have continued to do the work, carrying out God's ministry through teaching, healing and helping, as empowered by the Holy Spirit. Remember the revivals of the ages, crusades, rural evangelism and missionary outreaches across the world. Jesus wants us to do greater works than he did. We cannot downsize the work he wants us to do. He wants all of us to be powerful ministers in our different areas of calling. Jesus is not interested in doing the greatest works. Like a loving Father, he wants us to make impact as we live many years on earth.

2. "Whatever you ask in my name, I will do it…" (v. 13, 14). "We know He will answer our prayers when we walk in His footsteps" (1John 5:14).

This teaching takes us back to the Old Testament to consider the Israelites who knew God but constantly walked away from *the Way, the Truth and the Life*. From time to time, they went to the byways and were deceived, as is the case of many people, churches and nations today. The Israelites got stuck until they called on God.

One impactful story of the Old Testament is that of Deborah, the Judge. In Judges 4 and 5, we read about this woman, a wife, a mother and prophetess. In Judges 4:1, the children of Israel again did evil in the sight of God and ended up in the hands of an oppressor, King Jabin and, as expected, they cried out to the Lord. When they made the right choice, the most viable decision, God reached out to them. In verse 4, Deborah was introduced as a prophetess, wife of Lapidoth, a judge and a mother in Israel. We see that she judged under the palm trees, for people came to her for judgement. Deborah inspired Barak and they both went to war and won the battle with the assistance of another woman, Jael. The army commander of their enemies was killed by Jael. Here we learn the lessons of collaborative teamwork. Together, God used them to answer their national prayer. We cannot receive answers to prayers when we live in doubt and are not sure what we believe, especially if we are not united in purpose. In the story, we see the importance of collaboration, unity, and togetherness when led by God.

The very important person here is the man, Lapidoth, husband of the judge in the book of Judges. One would wonder what Lapidoth said when Deborah told him she was going to battle with Barak and the Israelite army. I also wonder what today's husband would have said. I am sure Lapidoth knew that Deborah was a prophetess and saw ahead of her time. He believed in her prowess and trusted that his wife would deliver by God's grace. "My heart is with the rulers of Israel, when the people willingly offered themselves. Bless the Lord" (v. 9).

You cannot offer yourself willingly to a person you do not know or one with whom you have no relationship. But victory calls for unity and willingness. Yes, the people made the wrong choice, made new gods to themselves and brought war on themselves. Just as Pharaoh and the Egyptians punished God's people and brought the plagues upon themselves, we bring punishment on ourselves when we refuse to obey God's command through a leader. Lapidoth recognized his wife's leadership role and that must have meant so much to her.

Let's always remember that Jesus Christ is the Way – "I am the Way, the Truth and the Life; no one comes to the Father except by me" (John 14:6). Again, it's time to look inwards because, obviously, our big names, knowledge, positions, titles and so forth have not helped us. Deborah was able to succeed because her husband was a secure man, who knew that the Lord had called his wife and was able to keep the homestead until she returned in victory.

The only thing that will matter in the end is our relationship with Jesus Christ and what we do in His name. Just like Deborah, Barak and Jael, the trio who led Israel to victory, we need to willingly follow the Way; we must work together to change our families and communities. We all need to consistently build our faith and that of our families.

Now is a wonderful time to grow in the Lord, beginning from our homes. Sometimes, it's hard but we are never giving up. As parents, we should continue our work of gathering together the family. As a couple, we should allow each other to shine for the Lord and support his calling on the lives of your spouse, just like Lapidoth did. It takes unity and trust to build a successful family life.

Once again, let's return willingly and follow the Way. Let's fulfil our calling, no matter the limitations. When God wants to use you, He will equip you. A peaceful and love-filled marriage is a tool in God's hands. So, look out for your spouse and stretch out your hands to have and to hold each other.

Chapter 17

NAKED AND NOT ASHAMED

Adam and Eve dwelt together and enjoyed each other's company. That was the intention of God when he created them, making them male and female. This helped them to live together in fellowship with one another and in communion with God. It was perfect.

> *And they were both naked, the man and his wife, and were not ashamed.* (Genesis 2:25)

The Christian marriage is meant to recapture that original state, when you truly marry a loved one, your best friend, a man or woman after your heart. If your spouse loves God, then you must endeavor to evoke the real joy of marriage. The married life becomes delightful and you'll experience the joy of marriage as ordained by God at the Garden of Eden. You come together to live in childlike sincerity and you are not planning to outwit or outshine each other. In a truthful relationship, you do not use empty words or flattery to get your spouse to do anything for you. To be yielded to each other, you have to surrender fully to God who watches over your home.

Like Adam and Eve, you are naked and not ashamed. God has instituted marriage for us to enjoy romance and sex in his full view, in a safe and holy estate. Are you taking advantage of this grace, freely given to you in marriage? You have the opportunity of playing together; but this does not last forever. So enjoy each other when you are still able to: "Let thy fountain be blessed: and rejoice with the wife of thy youth" (Proverbs 5:18). As the years go by, things change. If you truly love yourselves, the fondness continues to grow and get above and beyond sex. You will want to be together, even when one is too tired or sick or does not feel like it. You relive your youth continually and are there to support each other. Truly, you become inseparably glued together as one; your hearts are knit together by the power of love— the power of God.

Young couples ought to bond together and learn to play and build together. Let no one stand between the two of you. In-laws often try to come between couples. Some outsiders may report your spouse to you and tell you how more talented or versatile one is above the other. These are divisive intrigues that must be discountenanced as mischievous and evil.

Let your children and extended family members know that you are one and they will quit trying to show that they own any of you. They will come to respect your relationship and steer clear of trying to take sides. One thing family members find difficult to realize is that when a woman gets legally married into their kindred, she becomes a bona fide member of the family. No matter how much anyone wants to alienate her, she is engrafted into the entity with all the rights that accrue therefrom. The husband is supposed to ensure that his wife is fully integrated into the family and vice versa. If he is apologetic about the woman he married and makes her feel that she is not fully accepted, their marriage will continue to undergo tension.

There comes a time to let go. "Therefore, a man must leave his father and his mother and be joined to his wife and the two shall become one flesh... whatsoever God has joined together, let no man put asunder."

Okon always wanted to shield his wife from his family because he thought they were overbearing and would bother her. What he did was to relate to them as if Ima was not happy to accommodate them. Okon will hide and give them money and send messages to them behind Ima. When Okon was away from home, the family members thought Ima would not associate with them. Well, to their surprise and disbelief, she reached out to them. She visited them all, contributed to their needs and helped them even much more than Okon did. Some of the relatives were amazed and began to confess their earlier misconceptions. They became friendly and embraced Ima as family. You must integrate each other into both families for your love to keep growing. As much as you do not live with your parents, siblings, cousins and other extended family, they still play a major role in your relationship. It is necessary for them to see you as one and not be allowed to come in between. Hold your husband or wife; show affection that will amaze them and keep trotting together. Be open.

Again, what keeps you together? Many people dwell on their differences. They focus on their individual preferences and discover their selfish ends. We have more in common than differences. You can pray together, sing together, walk together, garden together, ride together, and sit out together. As you do these, you will laugh, learn, think, plan and even cry together. At the end of the day, you will lie together, play together and sleep together. It's not all about sex. Even then, sex is an honorable thing for couples to do in the presence of God. He has bound you together in the estate of matrimony. As you do all things together, you renew your youth and encourage yourselves.

It's about being fond of each other, tickling your spouse. Don't hide your sense of humor; enjoy each other's jokes. Remember the fun days, talk politics and watch your favorite movies and sitcoms together. Enjoy life together, "for it is your father's good pleasure to give you the kingdom." In the palace of your home, you are the king and queen. The husband's throne should be sacred for him. It could be a physical seat but it must be much more than that. It is a place of honor in the home. If you respect your husband, both of you are honored in the city. "As you make your bed, so you will lie on it." So, delight yourselves in each other and be open to one another at all times. Adam and Eve were naked and were not ashamed.

Chapter 18

MAKE YOUR MARRIAGE WORK

Mani graduated from one of the foremost universities in his tropical native land. He immediately got a well-paid job by the standards of his day. He was always hard-working and enthusiastic about life. In the course of time, Mani got married to Elizabeth, his classmate and longtime friend. The two worked together to build their home. However, the turnaround in the nation's economy began to beat hard on them. By the time their first child, Ekele was born, Elizabeth was still unemployed. That would not have meant so much if not that Mani's paycheck could no longer get them through the month. National inflation had encroached on them, so much that they now fed from hand to mouth.

As a supervisor on grade level 10 at the Board of Education, Mani loved his job and proudly looked forward to contributing to the educational sector and serving the nation. Of course, he also loved socializing with his team and colleagues and knew that he had prospects for growth, in spite of all odds. After a while, Elizabeth started to think about other ways to make money and contribute to the family income. As a graduate of sociology, she had applied to over thirty job openings but was not accepted in any. Joblessness stared her in the face.

With the birth of a child, they needed more money for feeding, clothing and baby needs. Meanwhile, they were tenants in a 2-bedroom apartment and would expect to grow out of it. Elizabeth's mother came to visit and stayed with them for some months to help her during the first weeks of childbirth. Mani and Elizabeth planned to make Mama comfortable. Yet, by the eighteenth day of the month, they were out of money and had no savings at all. Mani's next salary would come in ten or more days. That was the depressing reality.

When Mani came home from work that evening, he called Elizabeth into their bedroom and said, "You know, Honey, I had to go to 'South Africa' to help us cope this month," he said, smiling weakly.

"Dear, what do you mean by that?" Elizabeth was surprised and curious.

"Mr. Okon gave me the idea, so I swallowed my pride and did it!"

"You must be kidding!" she exclaimed, looking even more confused. Mani laughed loudly, looking lost; he then dropped a bunch of cash on the table.

"There you go! I took a salary advance from my workplace," he explained resignedly and sat down on the bed, watching his wife.

Elizabeth was both relieved and angry. Then she burst out crying. "So, it has come to this, Mani?" She felt defeated and sorry that, at this early stage of their marriage, they had to borrow money to get through the month. For the rest of the day, Elizabeth was planning for their future. She reflected on her family background, having come from a family of hardworking men and women, who could start a trade at any level. Her parents and grandparents never worked for anyone but were able to feed their children and educate them up to postsecondary levels. How much more herself with Mani who have had some solid foundation.

Three years later, when Neke their baby girl was born, Elizabeth was running two businesses: a provision store and a fashion design outfit. She had no need for a blue or white collar job. Mani was a grateful husband, who actively participated in the care of his children, unlike many of his colleagues. Together, they were economically stable by local standards.

All their children, Ekele, Neke, Buzi, Okey and Gani were born in Nigeria, in an era of dwindling economy and political turmoil. Everyone loved their family and their parents provided for them by dint of hard work.

On the Christmas Eve of 1996, Mazi Meke, their landlord came downstairs asking if Mani had returned from work. "No," said Elizabeth, "but I expect him to be back soon, since tomorrow is Christmas and we are leaving for the village later today," she explained.

"Please, let him know that his brother called from the US and wanted him to be at my house to take his call at 4pm today," he said.

"Thank you, Mazi," she replied.

Just as Mazi Meke left, Mani returned from work and, as usual, was excited to hear that his brother, Eze, had called.

"It's not often that Eze remembers to call me before Christmas," he was ecstatic.

At 4pm, he was already seated in Mazi's parlor. The call came through from his brother, Eze. Mani could hear his brother's hilarious voice bellowing from across the ocean like a trumpet of delight.

"Hello, Eze, my brother," Mani greeted in response.

The conversation was not long. But the message was profound. Eze told Mani that he got a letter informing him that Mani had won the Diversity Visa Lottery to the United States. In fact, the visa will ensure that Mani and his entire family relocated to the United States if they wanted to do so. And of course, why not?

Exhilarating was an understatement! Mani dropped the phone receiver, still rooted on his feet and overcome by emotions. He was grateful and happy.

He recalled when Eze came back home two years ago and mentioned the idea of filling out the visa lottery form. Even though they talked about it, Mani never followed up on it; and Eze did not tell him that he proceeded with the plan. Now, Mani was too dumbfounded to tell Mazi Meke any detail of the phone call.

When he got back home to his wife, it was overwhelmingly good news. Real Christmas gift for his family. 'America, here we come!' He imagined.

"Honey, there is a change of plan for us, "he started.

"Yes? What happened?" Elizabeth gazed at him.

"It's very good news for us all," he was beaming with smiles.

"What is it?" She was impatient.

"Eze just told me that we won the US Visa Lottery," he was breathless with joy.

"What are you telling me?!" She held her chest. "You are not serious!"

She pounced and flew into her husband's waiting arms. They were both overjoyed. The children soon got caught up in the jubilation, as they imagined themselves hopping on the flight to become American residents. "This calls for celebration, Liz!" Mani suggested.

"Yes! I agree. Let's start right now!" Elizabeth dashed into the kitchen and returned with soft drinks for everyone.

The road to America is never easy. The process of obtaining the physical papers to travel with a family of 8 was daunting, to say the least. After seventeen months, their Green Card packets were finally received. What about the flight tickets? Eze was ready to pay for four members of the family, but the other four also had to come along. The oldest child was eighteen, so it was necessary for him to go immediately. It took another six months to get everything set and the entire family was glad to join their folks in the white man's land.

Soon after they arrived in the US, Mani went to work like most of his peers. In order to fend for the family, he spent long hours at work and continued after work as a cab driver. His spiritual life suffered a great deal. He felt uprooted from the source of his strength. He was socially isolated. As things turned out, Elizabeth found a different peer group. She had returned to school to study to become a certified nurse assistant and went on to become a licensed practical nurse (LPN), while managing five of their children in a small apartment. While in school, she became friendly with a male course mate, Kanye, from another West African country; he became very friendly with her. Somehow, she didn't care about her husband any more.

Meanwhile, Mani was making a lot of money and sending to build a mansion in their native land. A few years after being disconnected from her husband, she became disrespectful of him, as she forged a relationship with Kanye. While in pursuit of the American dream, their children were totally neglected; each one took to the streets to fend for themselves.

When it became obvious that they had marital problems, friends, pastors and church members tried to intervene; but Elizabeth refused intervention. Mani got frustrated and, with time, his wife moved out of the house and moved in to live with Kanye. After ten years, Mani and Elizabeth still live in regrets. They lost their children to the system and daily regret ever stepping their feet on Newfoundland.

It is obvious that they forgot what was most important. God was no more the center of their family life. He used to be before their arrival in the US. By the second year after their arrival in Chicago, they had stopped praying together as a couple; they then stopped family prayers, forgetting that 'a family that prays together, stays together.' They forgot their root and paid dearly for that.

While Mani and Elizabeth were focused on making money, they lost sight of true prosperity, their children and the enduring legacy they had been building together for many years. When their pastor and church members tried to intervene, the two were carried away by selfishness and pride. Each one believed that they would make it better without the other.

Of course, Kanye eventually walked out of Elizabeth's life and married a younger woman. Elizabeth wanted to return to Mani, but he was already remarried to another woman, who used him like a mule. Every member of the family became frustrated and emotionally unstable. Their children were satisfied with the bare minimum. If only they had held to each other as they had vowed on their wedding day.

When parents are making the decision to end their marriage, it is important to consider the whole packet. Mani and Elizabeth should have remembered the following exhortation:

> But among you, as is proper among the saints, there must not be even a hint of sexual immorality, or of any kind of impurity, or of greed. Nor should there be obscenity, foolish talk, or crude joking, which are out of character, but rather thanksgiving. For of this you can be sure: No immoral, impure, or greedy person (that is, an idolater), has any inheritance in the kingdom of Christ and of God. (Ephesians 5:3 - 5)

A lot of people forget that God is watching them, even when they leave the place of their upbringing. And in the absence of prayer and spiritual fervor, there is a tendency to resemble the world and forget the outcome of disobedience to God. That is why Saint Paul's admonition includes the entire family in Ephesians 6:1 -3:

> Children, obey your parents in the Lord, for this is right. "Honor your father and mother" (which is the first commandment with a promise), "that it may go well with you and that you may have a long life on the earth." Fathers, do not provoke your children to wrath; instead, bring them up in the discipline and instruction of the Lord.

If only Elizabeth had remained the virtuous woman she used to be. If only the two focused on building together while remembering that God is in charge, whether in Africa or in the US. There are numerous examples of other couples, who have become spiritually deeper and more disciplined living abroad, including here in the US.

Example is the best teacher. Therefore, in order to truly mentor your children, you must remember to be the model of who you want them to be. Love your children, so you can bring them up in the instruction of the Lord. Remember to be in their lives so that your words will be impactful. If you are so selfish that you forget that you have children, you will live to regret your actions. Now that old age is beginning to slow her down, Elizabeth continues to beg for forgiveness and ask for help from those she refused to pick their calls in her younger years.

On the other hand, whenever Mani remembers their first love for each other and how he had neglected his family while chasing after money, he sheds tears. His new wife could never take the place of Elizabeth in his heart; he feels stuck in their relationship.

> "For the Lord God of Israel says that He hates divorce, for it covers one's garment with violence," says the Lord of hosts. "Therefore take heed to your spirit, that you do not deal treacherously." (Malachi 2:16)

Therefore, God is calling for reconciliation. Couples should not allow the foundation of their marriage to be eroded. Never look away from your marriage vows; rather, constantly remind yourselves how it all started.

> Since, then, we know what it is to fear the Lord, we try to persuade others. What we are is plain to God, and I hope it is also plain to your conscience…. And he has committed to us the message of reconciliation.

(2 Corinthians 5:11, 19b)

Chapter 19

WATCH THEREFORE

At that time the kingdom of heaven will be like ten virgins who took their lamps and went out to meet the bridegroom. Five of them were foolish and five were wise. The foolish ones took their lamps but did not take any oil with them. The wise ones, however, took oil in jars along with their lamps. The bridegroom was a long time in coming, and they all became drowsy and fell asleep. At midnight the cry rang out: 'Here's the bridegroom! Come out to meet him!' Then all the virgins woke up and trimmed their lamps. The foolish ones said to the wise, 'Give us some of your oil; our lamps are going out.' 'No,' they replied, 'there may not be enough for both us and you. Instead, go to those who sell oil and buy some for yourselves.' "But while they were on their way to buy the oil, the bridegroom arrived. The virgins who were ready went in with him to the wedding banquet. And the door was shut. "Later the others also came. 'Lord, Lord,' they said, 'open the door for us!' "But he replied, 'Truly I tell you, I don't know you.' "Therefore keep watch, because you do not know the day or the hour. Matthew 25: 1 – 13

The ten virgins had lamps and took oil in them. They were all waiting for the bridegroom. Then they all slumbered and slept. At midnight, the bridegroom arrived and they all received the call to go and welcome the bridegroom. The difference was that the wise took extra oil with them, but the foolish did not. While the wise could refuel and continue through the night, the foolish were exhausted and needed to go and buy oil. Meanwhile, they were out of time. The wise had the oil that will last them. Oil depicts anointing, power, and spiritual alertness. While their colleagues were out looking for oil, the wise went in to enjoy the presence of the bridegroom. That's the parable of the kingdom.

There will not be time to start praying for others, advising couples and friends when the trumpet sounds. This is the time for all to be empowered to run the individual race. Time to receive the anointing is now. Build a solid foundation for your marriage; a home that will support you in the midnight hour and strengthen you until the Lord's return.

Just like the five virgins who could not help their five friends, there will be a time you will not get responses from the prayer warriors. Each one will stand before the judgement seat of God and answer for him or herself. The foolish started running helter-skelter, looking for the anointing to continue. It was too late. It's like trying to make up for your marriage when you have already destroyed it. You've taken the oil out of it. You didn't take time to build a prayerful foundation. As they went seeking, the door was shut before they returned (verse 10). And the Master said to them, "Assuredly, I say to you, I do not know you," (verse 12). Will your negative attitude to your spouse be the reason why you run out of oil and return to the Lord too late? "Watch, therefore, for you know neither the day nor the hour in which the Son of Man is coming" (verse 13).

Watch, therefore! This is a call, a command, an admonition from our Lord Jesus Christ. Watch, because the Lord will come at an hour that you are not expecting. How do we watch? We must watch and pray. I have learned that there is emptiness in a prayerless believer. You need to pray enough and pray through. These are only experienced. I cannot tell you how to pray always, but the scriptures say, "Pray without ceasing" (1 Thessalonians 5:17). When you pray about every action you take, then you are praying enough. Pray in every situation and get response from the Lord, then you are praying through. You will receive your miracles and feel the surge of the Holy Spirit in you; "He that believeth on me, as the scripture hath said, out of his belly shall flow rivers of living water" (John 7:38). I feel it right in my belly during praise and worship—that is, the state that brings harmony in our relationships.

You must stay away from sin and love unconditionally. Your spouse is the greatest recipient of your joyous living. If you two pray together, you'll live in peace and love. When you watch and pray as a couple, you'll receive many miracles. You will pass together, touch God together and be victorious together. Watch and be ready. Be intimate with God and your spouse.

Chapter 20

WHAT WOULD YOU DO?

Experience is the best teacher, they say. Notwithstanding, the wise person learns from other people's mistakes. Here are some true life scenarios for discussion. These stories will help us realize that people make mistakes and can be wrong. Discuss the issues raised with your spouse or in small groups. Note what could be done differently for the best outcome of each case. Hold conversations and prayers that will strengthen your daily walk with each other.

1. Middle Age

Miriam stood out with her glistening white teeth. Her shapely slim figure made her outstandingly attractive among her peers. Yeah! Obi married the prettiest of them all and was always quick to compliment her for being the star of his life. She took care of her figure and worked out with her handsome husband as they enjoyed their youth.

Not so long after, the babies came: one, two, three, and their routine began to change. Miriam did her best to keep up with her lovely shape until she could no longer keep it. At one point, Obi could not hold her around her waist. The little figure 8 has gradually turned into figure 11. Obi was no longer the proud husband of the beauty queen. He began to complain about Miriam for her uncontrolled appetite. He was on his way out every evening after work. Of course, Miriam began to reminisce on how they started off together. It was clear to her that Obi liked her outward beauty and never really cared about inward virtue. Although he was a Christian, he often talked down on his friends for marrying ugly girls. He had not dealt with arrogance and never stopped to see that even his own stomach was beginning to protrude.

Miriam and Obi were beginning to rethink their marriage when we met. I talked to them about inner beauty and unconditional love. We looked at the before and after photos of other couples. It was obvious that no one remains looking the same over many years. I spoke to them about taking care of their bodies so that they remain attractive. Of course, you cannot give up on yourself and say, "Now I am old, so let him deal with it." Your dressing, cosmetics, body fragrance, hairdo and make up are meant to please your spouse and maintain your youth as long as you are able.

Of course, immodest appearance will only put a gentleman off. Together, you must work on improving your lives without attracting undue attention to yourself.

Questions for discussion

1. What scriptural advice will you give to Miriam and Obi on how to handle their situation?

2. How can they live in harmony while adapting to life's changes?

2. My Investment

Onu was quarreling with his wife, Chika and they went to see their pastor. After Chika reported about her husband's attitude towards her, the pastor asked him what his wife had done to deserve such treatment. Onu was quick to answer, "I married her and brought her to this country. Then I paid for her education. Now she is trying to be independent."

Pastor was confused and asked, "So, Onu what about that? Do you want her to be in bondage?"

"No, Pastor! You don't understand. My investment in her is not yielding fruit." He explained.

"Oh! Really. Is she not contributing to the welfare of your family?" Pastor probed, "What's the problem?"

Onu was still furious. He said he wanted Chika to be submissive, but she was not. She wanted to handle her own money. She did not allow him to control her spending any more.

There are only few of us who have given up on money. We do not allow money to possess us, whether we are husband or wife. In most successful marriages, at least one person has called money by its real name, mammon; and refused to let it rule his or her life.

Wherever both spouses are subjugated by money, they should read and meditate on the scriptures: "For the love of money is a root of all kinds of evil, for which some have strayed from the faith in their greediness, and pierced themselves through with many sorrows" (1 Timothy 6:10). Otherwise, evil would reign in their home.

Onu and his wife both loved money. He invested in her just to use her, but she also had her own intentions. As believers, they should have started by budgeting together, establishing a joint account for family use and designating investments for the rainy day. Then they can take off the hook of control from each other's use of their own money. The moment you begin to micromanage each other's earnings, the sooner suspicion creeps in and the two will fight over material and not substance. Substance is the spirituality that keeps you together. It is faith, "the substance of things hoped for, the evidence of things not seen" (Hebrews 11:1). I've known relationships where the husband is the chief accountant of the home, and others where the wife handles account. Some worked and others did not. A few couples have kept individual accounts and agreed on what amount to contribute to the center. Whichever method you agree on, I have discovered that you will have to still work on it by submitting your heart totally to God. Success lies in the state of the mind. If one or both of you feel insecure, then there will be problem.

Walk in love and have confidence in each other. If you are dishonest, of course, you cannot trust anyone else. An African adage says, "He who thinks of his own behavior will be calling another person a crook." That should not be the case if you have good intention for your marriage. If you begin to distrust your spouse or children, they begin to doubt you also. In the end, you will have your spouse and family turn against you.

Questions for discussion

1. What will be your advice to Onu and Chika to help them restore their relationship?

2. Suggest effective ways of handling family finances, giving examples from experience.

3. Phone Husband

Each time Osa returned home, he was on his cell phone talking with clients, friends, family members or other associates from far and near. He remained on his phone until he settled down to start watching the news on TV. In between, he may check his text messages and WhatsApp chats. His wife, Ndidi had already given up on him. She believed he was hooked on phone and social media. His loud conversations, hilarious laughter and hostility of his anger on the phone betrayed his emotional attachment to those on the other side.

As members of his household listened in on his conversations, one child or the other would glance at Ndidi, their mother, and say, "Mom, what do you think dad is talking about today?" or "Who are those people?" or yet, "How does dad get to know these kinds of people?" It became a dreaded pattern which they kept struggling to endure. It also became a rude interruption in their family life, which they would one day revolt against.

Questions for discussion

1. What do you think of Osa's social interactions?

2. How do you think this kind of behavior will affect the future of their marriage?

3. How best can Ndidi help her husband realize the vices in his attitude?

4. What phone and social media attitudes do you think this kind of person should adopt to improve his relationship at home?

4. Belonging

Nneoma has always wanted to be a celebrity. She wanted to be the Hollywood perfect wife and is dying to be on a reality show. Her husband, Frank is a simple, down to earth, hardworking family man with total devotion to his wife, family and career. The two are committed members of their church and fellowship. They had met soon after college during their service year and got married two years after.

Nneoma is a fashion freak; she got aligned to some classy middle-aged ladies in her church. Her friends were rich and could afford the changing trends of their day. These were ladies who could afford to travel locally and internationally and flaunt flamboyant cars. With time, Nneoma began to regard herself and Frank as living below poverty level. She complained about their meager resources and inability to afford life.

Frank tried to explain to her that they had to live within their means. Nneoma would not accept such suggestions and got angry. She started nagging and abusing her beloved husband. Although they loved each other and had been best of friends before marriage, their relationship began to deteriorate. Frank became subdued and was on the verge of depression. Yet, Nneoma was not relenting.

Questions for discussion

1. Do you think a marriage breakdown can be avoided in this situation?

2. Analyze the causes of Frank and Nneoma's disagreement.

3. Suggest what should be avoided before or during early marriage to avoid undue influence from friends and peers?

4. How can this couple avoid total anarchy? Use scriptural support to help them.

5. Best Friends

Latoya was new in town. She soon became best friends with Kay, who was battling a bitter divorce. Kay had established that her husband was maltreating and emotionally abusing her. She got the divorce and custody of her children. They were members of the same church and remained bosom friends until Kay's marriage got dissolved. Soon after Kay's divorce, Latoya began to have problems with her husband. Their young family began to face tough times. Their children watched them quarrel and fight on end. Latoya always ran out to take refuge with her friend and adviser, Kay.

Discussion questions

1. Do you think Latoya should remain friends with Kay?

2. What is the possibility of Latoya's marriage surviving?

3. Discuss how you will help her and her husband overcome their present challenges and succeed in their marriage.

6. Money Matters

Elaine is the custodian of her fathers' wealth; but her husband, Don complains of abject poverty in his own extended family. She also maintains her and Don's joint account. When his sister calls to make financial demands for the support of their mother who lives with her, Elaine refuses because she feels his family members are not hardworking. Don sometimes secretly sends money to his family; when Elaine finds out, she takes offence. Now they are fighting. He thinks she is too high-handed and uncompromising. She believes she's protecting her immediate family.

Questions for discussion

1. How do you think they can work things out?
2. What should be the place of money in that family?

7. Home Churches

After they got married, Julie refused to join her husband's church because her parents did not approve of her leaving her maiden family church. Julie and Frank lived like that for a while until their different network groups began to draw them apart. They came for counseling, realized their mistakes; she finally joined her husband's church and became a powerful instrument there. They made it work. However, Julie's parents are still not happy and are threatening to have nothing to do with her any longer.

Questions for discussion

1. What do you think their relationship with her parents should be?

2. Is it necessary for them to resolve this? If yes, how should this be done?

8. Different Doctrinal Convictions

After Nike and Bayo's separation, it was discovered that they both held unto different doctrinal beliefs and could not reconcile their views. They were still making effort to get back together, but could not agree on fundamental issues. Nike confessed that they had not prayed together for years; and that even when they did, Bayo felt she was noisy. He was often in a hurry to end the prayer session. Meanwhile, Nike thought they had not prayed enough.

Questions for discussion

1. Would you support their coming back to live together?

2. How can you advise them so they can have an enduring Christian relationship?

9. Child-centered Marriage

Maggie and Paul lived together because of their children who they had as soon as they got engaged. They actually wedded in order to keep the children in a matrimonial home. As the children grew up and left home, the two started to drift apart from each other. It seems they never learned to cleave.

Questions for discussion

1. How do you think they can work to enjoy living together?

2. Is it possible for the two to stay together successfully?

10. Vested Interests

Agnes was highly educated, had a great job, and was a beauty to behold. Her parents were also rich. Eke got engaged to her and once told her that the Lord had revealed to him how beautiful she would soon become. Agnes did not appreciate the non-complement and was wondering if that was meant to deflect her. She broke off the relationship, asserting that she wanted someone who loved her just as she was.

Questions for discussion

1. What do you think of the statement made by Eke?

2. Do you support Agnes' reason for ending their courtship?

3. What is the place of beauty in a relationship?

Chapter 21

WE VOWED

Have and hold your spouse as you promised at your wedding, before God and men. Although we are pressured on all sides and are often tempted to sway from our God-ordained path, "those who know their God shall be strong and do exploits" (Daniel 11:32b). Being strong is not based on physical might, but a resoluteness that comes from confidence in God. It is willingness to live by the word of God and loving our neighbors as ourselves. Just like taking a decision to live for Christ and going the extra mile to make it work, your marriage will work if you lay it on the altar of God's grace. Marriage is a reflection of our relationship with Christ, as exemplified in scriptures.

There are various experiences that can make you rethink your commitment to your spouse; but a prayerful individual will first talk it over with God. You will fight for your marriage and hold on tight because "a three-fold cord is not easily broken" (Ecclesiastes 4:12b).

Couples should never let anger rule over their lives. Each day's brawl should be settled before the end of that day, so that animosity will not pile up to yield disaster. There should be no doubt in your heart that you really love and care about each other.

As much as we love our children, we must not allow issues concerning them to divide us, lest our blessings turn into curses. Love your children, but be espoused to your husband or wife. Uphold each other's stand within the family, respecting and supporting the other even when outward beauty has faded due to age and health challenges.

In time past and even presently, the church has never taken divorce lightly. Of course, biblical teachings uphold marriage as one man and one woman, till they are separated by death. Nevertheless, many marriages (Christian and otherwise) of good and not-so-good people have ended in separation and, ultimately, divorce. The end of marriage is never sweet; it comes with guilt and could breed fear and bitterness. But in some extreme cases, divorce could be the only sane option in an unfeasible relationship. And when this happens, it is not the end of life.

However, before anyone embarks on terminating his or her marriage through divorce, all other options for reconciliation must be sincerely explored. The "Love Dare" challenge and devotional with the movie, "Fire Proof" (Kendrick, 2008) are great options for couples contemplating any form of separation or divorce. Going to your pastor or Christian counselors, along with attending prayer retreats must precede any final decision. At the end, if the Lord really ministers to your heart to come out from the marriage and be separate, then obey Him. "If God be for us, who can be against us?" (Romans 8:31b). If you are getting a divorce, you will need to continue with counseling and get prayer support, as you are in for a new phase of life. Never take it for granted, but be strong in the Lord, as he gets you through to either reconcile or adapt to the unexpected change.

This is calling on all Christian couples to uphold the integrity of the gospel through their marriages and family lives. They should maintain a daily time to pray together, schedule days to wait on the Lord together and uphold the family altar, which is a regular time to pray and study the Bible with the entire family. Bring up your children as a godly heritage. If as one, you establish a legacy of righteousness, you will stick together to enjoy it. When you invest in the life of your spouse, you will always be celebrating your mutual progress.

We vowed to hold onto each other. It is our duty to keep to our word. Like the call to humility, this is a call you must play a major part in. It is a call that hinges upon your integrity. Like the man who swears to his own hurt and does not change (Psalm 15:4b), strive to make your marriage work to the glory of God.

Bibliography

Kendrick, A. (Director). (2008). *Fireproof* [Motion Picture].

Kendrick, S. a. (2013). *The Love Dare: Day by Day.* Nashville: B&H Publishing Group.

Martin-Oguike, N. (2018). *Called Together.* Ibadan: BookMarkers.

Oguike, M. (2019, February 23). Family affair seminar. (S. P. Church, Interviewer)

Webster, M. (2020). *Merriam Webster Dictionary.* Retrieved from Merriam-Webster, https://www.merriam-webster.com/dictionary

Webster, M. (n.d.). *Dictionary.* Retrieved from www.merriam-webster.com.

Made in the USA
Middletown, DE
01 February 2023

22786836R00097